VINNIE HERE

Fanciful Conversations
Between
A Pastor and His Dog

Rev. Joseph Kraker & Vinnie

Illustrations by Judy Horn
Photos by David Shoenfelt

XULON PRESS

INTRODUCTION

V innie came to St. Vincent Church in Akron, Ohio as a six week old puppy. He had been thrown from a car and rescued by an observant driver, who turned him over to a pet rescue organization, "Home at Last." Soon after that, I was called by our school secretary, Mary Belany, and told she had a dog for me. I was unprepared and told her I didn't want a dog. My first dog, Timmie, (yes, I was at St. Timothy Parish then) had died recently and after 17 years with her, I wasn't sure I wanted to take on another long term relationship.

Not one to take no for an answer, I asked Mary to describe the puppy she had in mind. The description sounded very similar to my Timmie, and I asked her to bring the puppy to the parish house, so I could take a look at him. Hanging up the phone, I turned to Tim O'Rourke, our business manager, and said: "I think we have a dog." And in fact we did.

This five pound bundle of fluff, who now weighs in at 86 pounds of Lab mix, was irresistible, and it wasn't long before our newly named Vinnie had won the hearts of everybody in the parish, especially the children. Even today, people I don't even know will drive by us on our walks and shout from their car: "Hi, Vinnie," never bothering to say "hello" to me. But that's all right: "Love me, love my dog."

I had just finished reading the best selling "Marley and Me" when I happened on the idea of using Vinnie as a co-author of my weekly pastor's column: <u>Krumbs From the Kraker Barrel</u>. Pastor's columns can become rather tedious to produce and even more tedious to read, but our first installment, <u>Vinnie Here</u>, was a success, and suddenly parishioners were actually reading what I wrote. That was more than a year ago, and now I can't let Vinnie out of his commitment.

Vinnie has become a very popular co-author, and people look forward to reading about him each week. I try to capture his personality in what he says and the sometimes humorous ways in which he says it. This compilation of <u>Krumbs from the Kraker Barrel</u> is the result of requests I have had to bring them all together in book form.

Anybody who has a dog and therefore talks to his or her dog will appreciate the spirit in which these stories are written. Like me, you not only talk to your dog, but you also provide the dog's answers, and thus comes the dialogue. The one addition I have made in compiling these stories is the introductions, which show that I actually had a thought in mind each time I sat down to write. The discussion questions at the end of each story may prove helpful. If not, disregard them.

I want to thank Mary Belany for introducing us to Vinnie; Eileen Halaiko, our parish office manager, for retyping many of these pages and offering helpful suggestions; John Pressello for providing the graphics; Judy Horn for the drawings; Dave Shoenfelt for the photography; Sr. Jane Frances, Elizabeth Campbell, and Steve Halaiko for proofreading and correcting my mistakes; and all the parishioners of St. Vincent for encouraging me and being so kind to Vinnie.

VINNIE HERE

We have all experienced the pain of being rejected. Broken promises, faded dreams, loss of friends: all of these experiences leave us feeling alone and unwanted or unloved. When faced with these experiences, we need to hold on to the hope that there will be others who will love and accept us as we are. When the right person or persons come along, they are reminders to us of the love that God has for us. They are the angels in our lives who bear the message of God's enduring love.

The boss was really busy this week, so he asked if I could help out by doing his weekly message. I was only too glad to oblige, since the boss needs some help at times and there are a few things on my mind I would like to share with you.

I've noticed lately, maybe you have too, that books about dogs have had a lot of commercial success, bringing a healthy profit to the owners who wrote them. The last time I checked, <u>Marley and Me</u>, was among the top ten best sellers.

Well, what I've been wanting to tell the boss is that we could reap great financial gain for his/our retirement fund by writing a book about me. I'm every bit as smart as Marley, and a whole lot better looking too. The only problem might be that the boss can't write as well as Marley's boss, but I could help him with that.

Actually, I think people would be interested in reading about my experiences as a church dog. It's not every dog that gets to be a church dog. It is a very special calling and one which demands special skills, such as friendliness and, above all, gentleness. You can't be a church dog if you don't get along with people; and you certainly can't be a church dog if you're going to snap at children. You need patience to be a church dog.

Looking back on my own life, I am convinced that being thrown out of a car by someone who didn't want me was something meant to be. At the time it was pretty awful and I thought that my life was over. As it turned out, I was taken into a very nice home, with some pretty nice people, and I've never been without work to do and important work too.

I think if the boss would just tell some of those stories, people would find that my experiences are pretty much like their own. I've sat and listened to people telling the boss about how sometimes they feel like nobody wants them. Like me, they feel rejected and unwanted. But it doesn't have to be that way. God loves them, and someday, like me, they will find the person who brings God's love into their life. And then they'll know how great life can be.

I guess my life is meant to remind people of what the work of the Church is. I was plucked off the street and found a wonderful home here. Isn't that what Jesus came to do? We all need to be rescued and saved and then Jesus comes along like the lady driving in the car behind me. He picks us up, like she did, and finds a home for us. When people know my story, they will learn about their own story as well. That's what church dogs do. And that's what I wanted to tell you.

REFLECTION:

Recall the times you have experienced the pain of rejection or loss.

Call to mind the people who affirm you and accept you as you are.

Consider the importance of friendship and remember that to have a friend, you must be a friend.

Offer a prayer of forgiveness for those who have hurt you.

I was taken into a very nice home

THEY ALSO SERVE

Everybody is someone special, born with gifts and talents to be used in the service of others. Using our gifts simply to add to our treasure and aggrandize ourselves renders our gifts meaningless. God gave us our gifts to be shared with others in making this world a more perfect place to live. It doesn't come easily, but we can learn to let go of our own desires and discover the person that lies beneath. That is the person God intends us to be—a person for others. We must never worry that our gifts are unimportant. As John Milton reminded us: "They also serve who only stand and wait."

Look here, Vinnie, it says in this book that every dog has a special job to do. Some are shepherds and take care of the sheep, some are hunters.

So, what's your point, boss?

What is your job? What is your specialty? Excuse me if I haven't noticed, but I presume you have a gift that other dogs may not have.

Boy, boss, you sure are dense. Haven't you figured out what my specialty is?

Well, you're pretty good at begging, but I can't imagine that's what you were bred to do.

No, boss, that's something all dogs do as well as I, but you're getting warm.

You mean it has something to do with eating.

That's right, boss. Think about it.

There is one thing you do differently from my first dog, Timmie.

What's that?

When I would offer Timmie a treat, I had to be real quick, otherwise I might lose a finger. She would lunge at it, and sometimes get a piece of me along with the biscuit. You don't do that.

That's right, boss, I take it very gently, being careful not to bite down too hard. That's called having a soft mouth.

So what's that got to do with your job?

Don't you get it, boss? I'm a retriever. You shoot a duck and I'll swim out to retrieve it for you, so you don't have to get wet. It takes a soft mouth to do that kind of work. You wouldn't want me to bring you chopped duck.

That makes sense, Vinnie. That's why you run to get a toy for everyone who comes through the door?

Sure, boss. Since you haven't shot too many ducks lately, I have to bring whatever I can find.

All right, Vinnie, now I understand but I have a problem with that.

What's your problem, boss?

Well, it seems to me that if you're going to retrieve the ducks I shoot, you ought to drop them when you get to me. You don't do that. You hold on to whatever you have. What good is a duck, if I can't have it?

You've got a point there, boss. That's something I have to work on. Sometimes I forget that I'm supposed to be helping you. I have dreams of fricasseed duck, and I just can't resist keeping it for myself.

Maybe someday you'll learn to let it go, Vinnie, and then you will be the dog you were made to be.

I'm trying, boss. Some lessons take a lifetime to learn, so just be patient.

REFLECTION:

What gifts do I possess that could be used to help others?

Can I let go of the desire to use my gifts only for my own pleasure?

How could I use my gifts to serve others?

TO KNOW HOW TO WAIT

As a rule, we are not a very patient people. Many of us are Type A behavior people, the ones who watch for the yellow on the other side of the traffic light so we can get a good start. I once interviewed Dr. Friedman, the author of Type A Behavior and your Heart. *He taught me a valuable lesson about people like myself, whom he immediately identified as a Type A personality. He taught me the five year rule. When you get nervous about what you are experiencing, ask yourself: "what difference will this make in five years?" I find it helpful. I also find it helpful to fill up the waiting periods in my life with some meaningful activity. This is especially important when we consider our entire life is no more than a waiting period for the day we go to meet the Lord.*

What are you doing , Vinnie?

I'm waiting for you to come down, so we can go for our walk. It's that time of day, you know; time for us to take a hike.

I know, but I just had a call and now I have to visit the hospital. You stay here and I will be right back.

All right, boss, but don't dilly dally.

I'm back, Vinnie, where are you?

I'm over in the office, boss. I had some things to do while I was waiting for you.

Really? What have you been doing?

I've been taking care of the things I'm supposed to do.

Like what?

First, I had to help Eileen in the office. She's been working on the bulletin and I went in to offer her a little help.

What kind of help did you give her?

I could see she was working too hard, so I nestled in close to her so she could scratch my back and relieve some of her tension. I think it helped, because she gave me a biscuit for my efforts.

Great, I can see that was a selfless act on your part.

Always happy to be of assistance, boss.

What else did you do?

There were a few people who came to the door, and I had to greet them. You know how happy they are to see me, and if I'm not right there to give them a friendly "hello" they're awfully disappointed.

Did you know any of the people who came?

There were a few of the regulars. They're easy to deal with. They already know me, so I don't have to put on an especially big show for them.

Anybody else?

The cookie children were here. That requires a little more effort on my part.

What do you have to do special for them?

For starters, I have to take them over to the other door, where the cookies are kept. Then I have to make sure all the cookies get distributed evenly between the older children and the younger children.

Is that all?

No. Sometimes one of them drops a cookie and I have to clean it up. I'm telling you, boss, I've been very busy taking care of things while you were away. Isn't that what you told me to do?

Yes, Vinnie, you've done very well. Now we're ready for our walk. I'll go change and I'll be right down.

I'll be waiting, boss.

REFLECTION:

Are you a Type A person who finds it hard to be patient with delay?

Are you filling up the waiting period called life with meaningful activity?

She gave me a biscuit for my efforts

DON'T FORGET YOUR HEART PILL

Many are aware of the need to take care of their physical health, and some go to great pains to do so. The sale of vitamins, not to mention drugs, together with health clubs is testimony to the great concern we have for remaining healthy. The soul also needs attention, since there are viruses that can creep into the soul and lead to spiritual illness. To ward off these potential dangers, a regimen of spiritual exercises is necessary, including prayer, spiritual reading, and a regular reception of the sacraments.

What's that big thing in my food bowl, boss? It looks funny.

That's your heart pill, Vinnie.

What's wrong with my heart? I thought I had a pretty healthy heart.

You do, Vinnie, but you need to keep it that way.

You mean there's a danger something might happen to my heart if I don't swallow that big pill?

That's right, Vinnie. You may develop heart worms.

Heart worms! That sounds terrible. I don't want any worms crawling around inside my heart.

It's worse than that Vinnie, they could actually get to be so many and so big that they would keep your heart from working, and you know what that would mean.

Ugh! What's that pill going to do?

That's going to knock off the little buggers before they get a chance to grow.

How do they get into my heart to begin with? I never invited them in.

They come from the mosquitoes that bite you. They get into your blood and then into your heart.

Do you have to take a heart pill too, boss?

Well, not exactly like yours, but I do have to watch what gets into my heart. My heart stands for the things I think about and all the things I would like to do. If I start thinking wrong thoughts or think about things I know I shouldn't do, then you might say I had heart worms.

Where do your heart worms come from, boss? Mosquitoes?

Kind of. They come from being around the wrong kind of people. People who put bad thoughts in my mind and the next thing you know, I'm agreeing with them. Sometimes they come from the kind of world I live in. There are a lot of temptations in our world, and if I let those temptations into my heart, it grows sick.

Do you have a pill for that, boss?

Oh yes. I take several pills to prevent my heart from getting sick. One pill is prayer, another is Holy Communion, and there's another called spiritual reading. I take one a day and they keep my heart from getting sick.

What do you do if one of those worms gets into your heart? How do you get rid of it?

I have a really powerful pill for that, called Reconciliation. It knocks that worm right out of me.

I wish I had as many kinds of pills as you do, boss. Mine tastes pretty good and I could use a few more.

REFLECTION:

Do I have a time set aside each day for prayer and spiritual reading?

How often do I receive the sacraments, especially Holy Communion?

What are some of the temptations I face in the world around me?

BURYING BONES

Retirement plans are good, and leaving something for our children is good, but how much, that's the question. If saving money becomes an obsession, it narrows the possibilities of helping those who are presently in need. If one is fortunate enough to acquire a healthy sum of money in the course of their life, then a decision needs to be made concerning how much of that money is given to assist people in need. The biblical practice of tithing is a practical way to resolve that issue. The biblical tithe was ten percent. If that seems too high, we are free to determine what best fits our circumstances.

What is that thing you just brought into the house, Vinnie? It looks disgusting.

To tell you the truth, boss, it is disgusting. It's a bone I buried out in the yard a long time ago. I guess it didn't age very well.

You can say that again, Vinnie. Take that thing out of here before it smells up the house.

Sorry about that, boss. That was a really good bone when you gave it to me. I just wanted to save it for later. You know: that rainy day thing.

Turns out it saw too many rainy days, Vinnie, and now it's rotten and covered with dirt.

You know I buried the bone just in case the day came when I wouldn't have anything to eat.

There you go, that's the problem: you just didn't have any faith in me. You know I always give you enough to eat, but you doubted, and now look, you've lost a really good bone.

I'll have to remember that the next time.

Don't feel too bad, Vinnie, people do the same thing.

Do people bury bones, boss?

In a way they do, Vinnie. People sometimes have more money than they need, so they salt it away. That's a good thing, up to a point, because we live a little longer than you, and we have to be ready for the day we can't work anymore. We need to have some money saved up for the future.

Does it look like my bone when you go to use it?

No, not exactly, but it can become a problem.

What happens to it, boss?

Sometimes we make the same mistake as you. We don't have enough trust that God will continue to provide for us, so we put away so much money that we will never be able to use it all.

What's wrong with that, boss? It's your money.

Yes, but there are so many people who have so little, that it would be better to share it with them. After all how much money does a person need?

You know what's going to happen to all that money, boss?

No, what?

It's going to be like my bone, and someday their Boss is going to tell those people just what you told me. He's going to tell them to take that messy money and get out of his house.

You may be right, Vinnie.

Can I have a new bone, boss, since this one is no good anymore?

What for?

I want to give it to a poor friend of mine.

REFLECTION:

Do I use the excuse of saving up for a rainy day to keep from sharing with others?

Am I perhaps too cautious in spending what I have, afraid to let go of anything?

What percentage of my income can I afford to share, even if it hurts a little?

AWAY, BUT NOT GONE

When Jesus left this earth, he left behind his followers who would continue his work of teaching and healing. We live in the in-between time of Jesus' departure and return. During this time we try to remain close to Jesus by recalling the things he said and did, always striving to deepen our relationship with him. The best way to strengthen our relationship with the Lord is by striving to live as he lived, walking in his footsteps and doing the work he has assigned to us. If we remain faithful, we hope to receive an eternal reward when the journey of life is over.

Yo, Vinnie, I'm home!

All right, boss, that's good. I've been waiting for you all day.

But you knew this was my day away.

Yes, I knew that, you told me enough times, but that doesn't make it any better.

I've been told that when I'm away, you just lie around and mope all day. Is that true?

Well, not exactly, boss.

Then what do you do?

It's like this, boss. I look for the things that remind me of you. That way it seems like you're here, even if you're gone. Does that make any sense?

I guess, but give me some examples.

For example, I walk around and sniff your footprints. That way I can pretend you're still here, and you don't seem so far away.

Yes, I can understand that, Vinnie. We humans do pretty much the same thing.

You mean you go around smelling footprints?

No, of course not. But we try to relive the moments we have spent with others by going back and remembering the things we did together. We like to retrace our steps. It helps us remember the people who aren't with us anymore.

That's neat, boss. I thought we dogs were the only ones who did that.

So, what else do you do? You can't walk around sniffing the carpet all day.

No. that's just one way I fill up the time, but I have found an even better way.

What's that?

I make up my mind that you're not going to be home for a while, so I try to make up for it by doing the things you would do, if you were here.

No kidding, how do you do that?

Oh, it's easy. I keep listening for the doorbell so I can go to the door and greet people when they come.

That's good, what else?

I find the best thing is helping out. For example, when the children come, I make sure they get their treats, just like you do. When I do what you do, it's as if you were here.

Amen to that, Vinnie. You are filling in for me, and even if I am gone, I am still here, because you are taking my place. That's just what I would want you to do.

Exactly, boss. And the best part is when you come home and bring me a treat. By the way, that's enough jibber-jabber, where's my treat?

REFLECTION:

Do I devote time each day to spiritual reading and meditation?

Am I aware of the work God has assigned to me?

What are some of the ways I can participate in the work of Jesus?

The best part is when you come home

LIFE-GIVING FOOD

When it comes to nourishing the spirit, there are some things helpful for us and others which are not. Some of what we feed our spirit is actually harmful — junk food for the soul. It's available everywhere, like chicken bones on the street. It's in our homes via television and the internet. It's in the marketplace in theatres and book stores. The first step toward spiritual help is to avoid such junk food. The second step is to find nourishment in our spiritual reading, prayer and, most of all, the sacraments.

What's the matter, Vinnie, you appear to be rather listless.

I'm just a little tired, boss. I'll be all right.

I don't know, Vinnie. Let me see. Ah-ha, just as I thought. Your nose is dry and warm. Are you sure you're all right?

To tell you the truth, boss, I've been a little concerned about that. I was reading this morning about all that bad dog food they've been selling, and I was wondering if I may have eaten some.

Yes, I saw that too, Vinnie, and your brand of food is listed as one of the infected ones.

Ohhhhh, just as I feared. I've been poisoned!

Now, wait a minute, Vinnie. Let's not jump to conclusions. You've eaten a lot worse things than your dog food.

I have?

Sure. Just yesterday you grabbed an old chicken bone off the street. Who knows where that came from and how long it had been lying there. Besides that, you're not even supposed to eat fresh chicken bones.

Yea, right. I had forgotten about that.

And how about those doughnuts you take from people who come to the house for First Friday doughnuts and coffee?

But I have to take those. Nobody ever gives me one. How else am I supposed to get one?

That's just the point. You're not supposed to get one. They aren't good for you.

I know, but they sure are good. And besides, they're not good for you either.

Have you ever seen me eating one?

Oh, you're just so perfect, you're boring. So you don't think I'm suffering from food poisoning?

I'm sure you aren't, Vinnie. I read the paper also, and I called to make sure your food wasn't infected.

I'm glad to hear that, boss. I was beginning to worry that I might have to cut down on my diet.

That might not be a bad idea, but you don't have to do it by giving up the food you're supposed to eat. You might want to cut out some of the junk food.

I'll think about that, boss. But thanks for looking into things for me. I appreciate your concern.

You're welcome, Vinnie. You should know I wouldn't let you have something that wasn't good for you.

I know, boss. The food you provide is really the best of all.

REFLECTION:

How carefully do I avoid the junk food that surrounds me?

What sources do I have for spiritual nourishment that satisfies?

Have I engaged in any spiritual reading lately?

FIFTEEN MINUTES

Why is it that people enjoy seeing themselves in the news? Whether it's in a local publication or on television news, our reaction is always the same and we want everybody to "come and watch; I'm going to be on television." Andy Warhol's well known quotation was said in reference to the ubiquitous nature of modern media, which will someday touch every one, as it did Vinnie. Perhaps receiving recognition affirms our belief that our lives are important. But most of us, like Wordsworth's Lucy, dwell "among the untrodden ways," and never receive widespread recognition. No matter, we find happiness and satisfaction in knowing that our life meant something to someone.

Well, Vinnie, that was some article about you in the Akron Beacon Journal. What did you think about it?

Oh, it's nothing, boss. Giving interviews and posing for pictures is all in a day's work for a church dog. It goes right along with answering the door and greeting visitors.

Yes, but it's not every dog that gets its picture in the paper. That must make you feel pretty proud.

Not really, boss. It's like Andy Warhol said: "In the future everyone will be famous for fifteen minutes." We all get our fifteen minutes on the stage and then it's over and we go back to living ordinary lives.

I know Andy said that, but it's not really true is it? I mean there are a lot of people and a lot of dogs who don't even get their fifteen minutes. You got yours, but think of all the dogs out there that live lives of quiet desperation.

Quiet desperation? Where did you get that boss?

Henry David Thoreau said it: "The mass of men lead lives of quiet desperation. What is called resignation is confirmed desperation."

I'm not sure I agree with him about that. He must have been a bit of a loner. Did he live all by himself?

Well, I guess he did part of the time. There was a little pond outside of Boston where he spent a lot of time observing life.

I think I read about that. Walden Pond, wasn't it?

That's right. I spent a whole afternoon once looking for the place. It isn't much and nobody who lives near it seems to even know about it.

That explains it, boss. The man spent too much time out there watching the grass grow. He didn't know that there is more to life than trying to figure it out.

So, what advice would you have given Henry?

I would have told him to get a life. Go out and meet people the way I do, then he would have discovered that there is great satisfaction in helping others and bringing some happiness into their lives.

Do you think he would have changed his mind if he had you around?

Absolutely, boss. I would have showed him that there is no such thing as a life of quiet desperation, if you fill up your life with acts of kindness. Nothing is as meaningful and satisfying as that.

Sometimes you can be brilliant, Vinnie. You amaze me with your wisdom and insight. It's no wonder you were chosen to be the subject of such a nice article.

As I said, boss, it's nothing. Stick with me and you too will get your fifteen minutes of fame.

REFLECTION:

What, if any, was your moment in the sun?

Why do people enjoy reading about themselves or seeing their picture in the paper?

What are you doing with your life that makes it meaningful and fulfilling?

FRIENDS WITH EVERYBODY

Passing judgment is a fault most people have trouble trying to get over. There are so many prejudices, some of which are personal and others which are inherited. Societal prejudice is especially harmful. It keeps some from having an opportunity to exercise their gifts and better their lives. Racism in particular has been an ugly blemish on American life. It will take each of us a lifetime to conquer it, and then we can only confess that we are "recovering racists," because it keeps finding new ways to insert itself. Abandoning prejudice of every kind is a goal we must constantly seek to attain.

Oh boy, Vinnie, do you see what I see?

I sure do, boss. Look at all those dogs up there ahead of us. Count'em, there are five of them.

Yes there are. That man has his hands full. Imagine walking five dogs at once. He must be a professional dog walker.

I don't know about that, boss, but could you step it up a little? I want to catch up with them before they get away from us.

I'm walking as fast as I can, Vinnie. Take it easy. We'll catch them, but I don't know what's going to happen when we do. I kind of wish they would find someplace else to walk.

Trust me, boss, I'll behave like a real gentleman.

Yeah, Vinnie, but your idea of gentleman is different from mine. Do you always have to be so very friendly?

You know me, boss, always the friendly pooch.

Oh, look at that, Vinnie, they're turning into the cemetery. What a shame, we're going to miss catching up with them. Too bad.

Do I note a hint of glee in your voice, boss?

Look at them over there, boss. Too bad they have this fence around the cemetery. Now they can't even get over to see me.

That's the reason for the fence, Vinnie. It's for everyone's safety. Uh-oh, wait a minute. That one little guy has been able to crawl under the fence.

Yes, boss. Let's give him a minute to get over here.

Hi. My name is Elvis.

Nice to meet you, my name is Vinnie, and this guy is the boss.

Glad to meet you, Elvis, but don't you think you should crawl back under that fence and go with the other dogs you came with? I don't want you rushing out into the street. You may get hurt.

You're right, sir. I just wanted to say "hello" to this beautiful dog of yours.

Thanks, Elvis, goodbye.

Poor Elvis, Vinnie. He wasn't the most handsome dog I've ever seen. He was kind of too short and a little over weight. But I'm proud of you, Vinnie, you treated him just like all the other dogs you meet. I have to hand it to you, Vinnie, you treat all your friends the same.

That's the way it should be, boss. It doesn't make any difference how they look or how much they have, we dogs treat everybody the same. You guys could learn from us.

We're trying, Vinnie. Keep reminding us.

REFLECTION:

Am I aware of any prejudices in my life?

Do I constantly seek to understand better those whom I may pre-judge?

Have I made any conscious effort to reach out to those who are different from me?

We dogs treat everybody the same.

THE STOCKINGS
WERE HUNG

*There is something very ironic about the way we cele-
brate the birthday of Jesus. He spent his whole life
caring for those who were considered the outcasts of
society. He had a special place for those whom others
shunned: tax collectors, widows, sinful women, the
blind and the lame. Our celebration of Christmas is
too often spent in finding the right gift for the person
who has everything. It would make more sense for us
to focus on the life and message of Jesus, using, as
many do, this time as an opportunity to help others,
not only at Christmas, but throughout the year.*

What are you looking at, Vinnie?

Oh, I'm just lying here on the living room
carpet and looking at the mantle.

Did you see your stockings hanging there?

I sure did. I'm waiting for them to be filled.

Have you told Santa what you would like in your
stockings this year?

I've been thinking of that, boss. You know it gets harder each year to think of something I need.

I can surely understand that. You already have just about everything.

I suppose you're right, boss. I don't know if I need any more toys. I've got plenty of those, but I can always use a few more rawhide chews or dog biscuits. One can never have enough of those.

That's debatable, Vinnie. From the looks of you, you're not exactly starving.

No I'm not, but I still like those things, although as I grow older, I have less interest in them than I used to.

So why are you staring at the mantle? What is it that seems so interesting to you?

It's so different at this time of year. All those figures you have up there. I'm trying to figure out what's going on. It's obviously something very important.

Yes it is, Vinnie. That stable and all those figures represent the night that Jesus was born.

Well, that explains it. I was wondering who that little baby was. But boss, if that's Jesus, couldn't he have picked a better place to be born than in a stable?

I'm sure he could have, but he chose a stable, because there was no room for him at the inn, and Joseph had to find a place fast. All he could find was a stable.

You know, I really like that, boss. Just think; if I had been there I would have felt right at home with all the other animals.

Yes, you would have, Vinnie. As a matter of fact, if you look closely, you'll see a black dog, just like yourself, sitting right next to the baby Jesus. I put him there, because I knew that's what you would do.

Wow! That's great, boss. Now I'm beginning to appreciate Jesus' birth even more. Just think, he wasn't too big to allow even people like me to be near him.

He preferred people like you, Vinnie. Now, how about a little Christmas snack?

Later, boss. I think I'll stay here and keep an eye on the baby Jesus this Christmas.

REFLECTION:

Is Christmas for me a spiritual or a secular celebration?

Could I cut back on the amount of money I spend on gifts to have more money to help the poor?

Who are some of the people in my city or town that need help?

LETTING GO

We all have more than we need, and a visit to your local Goodwill or Salvation Army thrift shop will convince you of that. Most of us are pretty good about giving away items we no longer use or need, but the heart of charitable giving consists not only in letting go of things we no longer want, but also in giving from what we depend on. The Bible promises that we will receive generously in return for what we give, but the real reason for giving is to imitate the generosity of God, who lets his rain fall on the good and the bad.

Vinnie, this toy box of yours is getting too small.

You know, boss, ever since I was a puppy and had that puppy shower, people have been bringing me toys. I guess you'll just have to get a bigger box.

You know, there's another solution to this problem, Vinnie. We could get rid of some of these toys. You could keep some of your favorites like the Cat in the Hat, or the monkey with long arms.

But what about my little puppy and the fake pieces of sheep skin? You can't throw those out.

Well, how many toys do you need?

Keep in mind, boss, they are the tools of my trade. It's my job to greet people at the door and then run to get a toy to play with. Those toys are very useful.

I get the impression, Vinnie, that you don't want to let go of any of them.

I'd rather not, boss.

You know, I don't think I would mind so much if only you would learn to pick up after yourself. Every morning I have to go through the house cleaning up after you. You just let your toys lie wherever you want.

It's better that way, boss. I like to have my toys spread out around the house where I can conveniently find them.

But that drives me crazy, Vinnie. You know I like to have everything where it belongs.

Can I help it if you're a neat freak, boss?

Well, I still think we should get rid of some of these toys. You could share them with some other dogs that don't have as much.

That's easy for you to say, boss, but I notice you aren't so good at sharing yourself. I don't see you sharing when you have a plate full of food and I'm sitting there with nothing. A little good example would go a long way.

But that's for your own good, Vinnie. My food isn't good for you.

Well, maybe you're right, boss. But you have to admit that people have just as much trouble letting go of things as I do.

I will admit that much, Vinnie. It seems we have that problem in common.

So let me think about it, boss. I know there are some other dogs around here that don't have as much as I. Maybe I'll start giving some of these toys to them.

Good idea, Vinnie. And don't forget that the hand that gives, gathers.

That may be, boss, but what I give will be freely given. No strings attached.

REFLECTION:

Take notice of all the things you have which you don't need or use.

Ask yourself if you ever really needed them. If not, why did you buy them?

Is it time to do some spring cleaning, sharing what you have with others?

HE LIVES

The celebration of Easter is filled with hope that even the worst moments of our lives are able to be redeemed, because there is a Father in heaven who watches over us and will lift us from our times of defeat. Serious, life-threatening illness can leave us feeling lost and alone. The look and touch of a friend can reassure us and restore our faith in God. When life bears down on us like a speeding car and threatens to destroy all that is good, we must know it is not the end and that good times will return.

What's that you're eating, boss?

It's an egg, Vinnie.

I never saw a blue egg before.

That's because this is an Easter egg.

What's so special about an Easter egg, boss?

This egg represents Jesus rising from the tomb to new life. Just like a new born chick comes from an egg, so Jesus came forth from the tomb on Easter morning. He rose from death to life.

I can understand that, boss. I once did something like that myself.

You did?

Yes. Remember that time, when I was young and foolish. I didn't know how to listen and I ran across Market St. one Sunday morning while you were locking the church.

How could I forget? You ran across the street, and luckily there were no cars coming, so you were all right. I ran after you to make sure you got home safely, and you thought I was playing with you, so you ran back, but this time you weren't so lucky. There was a car coming at a pretty good clip and hit you hard on the head.

I could've been killed, boss.

I thought you were dead, Vinnie. You just laid there in the street, not moving and bleeding from your mouth. I thought for sure your young life was over. I picked you up and carried you back to the house.

I kind of remember that, boss. I remember you carrying me. I remember opening my eyes and looking up at you, and that's when I knew I was going to be all right.

How could you be so sure of that, Vinnie?

Because I knew you were there with me and that you wouldn't let anything happen to me.

Well, Vinnie, you're right about that. And that's how Jesus must have felt the day he died. He always knew his Father was close to him. He may have wondered where his Father was on the day he died, but he knew his Father would take care of him, so he simply placed his life in his father's hands and died.

So did his Father raise him up, boss?

He sure did, Vinnie, on Easter Sunday. That's what we're celebrating today, because we know the Father will raise us up too, just as he did Jesus.

That's great, boss. We ought to celebrate. Hand me one of those red eggs.

REFLECTION:

Have I ever felt like I had been run over by a car and all was lost?

What happened to restore my spirits?

Do I really believe that even in death there is hope of new life?

Pray often: "Lord, I do believe, help my unbelief."

We ought to celebrate

SPRING'S ETERNAL HOPE

Adversity is a part of life, but it is never welcome. That is not to say it doesn't have it's place. Hard times can be very effective teachers. Hard times not only teach us to appreciate the better times, but they also serve as powerful reminders of our need for God's assistance. We pray to God for help in such times, and it seems that our prayers may go unanswered. However, patience will bring its own rewards and God will be found faithful to his promises. We must learn that God's time may not be the same as our time, but God is always "on time."

Did you hear that, boss?

Did I hear what, Vinnie?

That bird, boss. It's the red, red robin, come bob, bob, bobbin' around.

Yes, you're right, Vinnie. That sure is a welcome sound isn't it? We haven't heard that since last summer.

No we haven't, and this year I'm more ready for it than ever. These last few weeks have been brutal.

It's good to hear the song of a robin in the morning. It's a harbinger of better days to come.

I guess, you're right, Vinnie. It has been a little rough with all the cold weather and wind, not to mention the snow. I'll be happy when we have some sidewalks to walk on again. I don't like walking in the street.

I'm with you there, boss.

Did you think this day would ever come, Vinnie?

Well, it was a long time coming, but I guess I knew the grass would get green and the trees would sprout leaves again. After all this isn't the first time we have gone through the difficult days of winter.

Yes, I think I knew it too, Vinnie. I've been through a lot more winters than you, and I've never known one that didn't end in spring.

That's a good way of putting it, boss, but isn't it funny?

What's funny?

How we know winter isn't going to last forever, but we still worry about the weather and wonder when it's going to change.

You're right, Vinnie. It seems that the robin knows more than we do. He knows when the winter is going to end and he shows up right on time.

I'll have to remember that, boss. The bad times go away, just like everything else, and I must learn to be patient and wait for better days.

That's right, Vinnie. Sometimes God's time is different than ours, but God is always on time.

Come to think of it, boss, maybe the bad times are necessary.

Really?

Yes, just think, boss, if we hadn't had so much bad weather, we wouldn't have noticed that robin singing. We would have taken it for granted.

By golly, you've got something there, Vinnie. Does that mean the bad times are really good times?

Don't bother me with such silly questions now, boss. Just listen to the robin singing.

REFLECTIONS:

What are some of the things I complain about?

Are there reasons these things may be good for me?

Am I patient in waiting for "God's time" to be fulfilled?

GETTING ALONG

There may be some who get along with everyone, but for most of us it's not that easy. Sometimes people just bother us for no other reason but that they annoy us. Others may have hurt us in the past and now we have trouble forgiving and forgetting, especially the latter. In the worst case scenario we may want to get even; short of that we may just decide not to associate with these people any more than is necessary, which makes for a pretty frosty relationship. This can be especially distressing when the person involved is a family member. In the long run, it is best to put hurts and petty annoyances behind us. To do so makes us winners, with peace of mind and heart the reward.

Hey, Vinnie, look at that ragged looking dog in the field over there. That poor fellow looks like he's had a really bad day.

Holy cow, boss, you'd better stay away from that guy.

Why do you say that, Vinnie?

Because, boss, that's not a dog.

It sure looks like a dog to me.

He may look like a dog, but he's not. He's a coyote.

No kidding, you mean like the one in the movies?

I don't know about that, boss, but it's better that we don't find out.

Are these coyotes dangerous, Vinnie?

They are if you're a smaller dog than I am. They like to feast on smaller animals and they can be a problem for people with small pets like little dogs or cats.

Do they ever attack people like me?

Not ordinarily, boss, but now that they are getting accustomed to being around you guys, they seem to have lost their fear of you, and so I wouldn't get too friendly if I were you.

You'll have to admit, Vinnie, that he looks quite a bit like you.

Of course he does, boss. After all we are distant cousins. But we dogs learned long ago how to get along with humans like you. It took some doing, but we finally figured it out. The first real dog, we call him "Ur-dog," learned that when it comes to getting along with humans, you catch more flies with honey than with vinegar.

It would be interesting to know how Ur-dog learned that lesson.

None of us knows for certain, boss, but there is a legend among us dogs that Ur-dog was out hunting one day when he came across one of you humans cooking a chicken on an open fire. He was tempted to do what dogs had always done until then.

What was that, Vinnie?

Well, he was going to attack the human and after chasing him away from the food, Ur-dog would have had it all to himself.

So, what happened?

Well, he heard this human calling him, saying things like: "nice doggie" or "here boy." So Ur-dog went over to the man and the man handed him a bone. That's how the story goes, and ever since we have been your best friends. We dogs have a saying: "The best way to conquer an enemy is to make him your friend."

I thought Abraham Lincoln said that.

He must have had a dog.

REFLECTION:

1. Who are the people I have trouble getting along with?
2. How do I treat these people?
3. Is it possible they could become my friend?

THIS IS LIVING

There is so much in life we should celebrate, and too little time to do so. Staying anchored in God helps us appreciate just how precious life is, and how hard we should work to protect it. How sad that so many are deprived of the opportunity to experience the joy of living. For some this right is stolen before they are born, for others it is a condition that blinds them to life's pleasures. We must pray for all who have not known life as a blessing and a cause for rejoicing.

What's with the two bowls of food today, boss? Is this my birthday or something?

No, Vinnie, we're going to participate in a taste test to determine which of the two foods you like the most, your old one or the new one.

That's sure a whole lot better than the tests I get at the doctor's office. No pins or needles, no poking and probing, no scales and thermometers—just food. Now that's what I call a test. What do I have to do?

There's nothing to it, Vinnie, you just decide which one you want to eat first. I will presume that is the one you prefer, since you've never been one to save the best for last.

Boss, dogs can't afford to save the best for last. When you're a dog and food is hard to come by, you eat what you can, when you can. Saving the best for last is for those who have everything they need and don't have to worry about losing the little they have.

Thanks for the reminder, Vinnie. Sometimes I forget what it is like to be always looking for food.

Don't mention it, boss. I'm always happy to be of assistance. Now, let's get on with this taste test.

Go ahead, Vinnie, I'll observe.

Hmmm, this one smells pretty good, but wait, let me smell the other one. Hmmm, that one smells good too. Let me try that again. Hmmm, hold on a few moments while I bask in the aroma.

Well, which one is it, Vinnie? You have to make up your mind.

Don't rush me, boss. This is an opportunity that doesn't come too often. I have to make the most of it.

Take your time, Vinnie, I'll wait.

OK, boss, I've decided. It's the new one.

What made you choose that one, Vinnie?

It just smelled better. More of the kinds of things I like to eat. I won't mention what they are; you might become ill.

Well, I'm glad you chose the one you did.

You are?

Yes, because I think that one will be better for you. It gives you all the things you need and it's especially formulated for senior dogs. It should make you feel better.

You didn't have to mention that senior dog thing, but you're right, I think I feel better already. I feel like going out and tackling the world.

That's the Vinnie I like to see, fully alive and kicking.

You've got it, boss. I feel like I have a whole new life. Come on, let's go out and celebrate life!

REFECTION:

Am I a person who generally appreciates life?

What do I do on those days when life is not so beautiful?

How can I contribute to promoting the gift of life for others?

Dogs can't afford to save the best for last

THINGS CHANGE

No one likes change, but things do change. The world we live in changes and we change as we grow older. Learning to adapt to these changes is an art which demands we hold on to the things that matter, and let go of those that don't. The letting go is part of our spiritual growth. It is God's way of drawing us away from the world we live in, and closer to himself. In the language of the spiritual masters, it is called self-denial or mortification: an emptying out of ourselves to make room for God.

What are you waiting for, Vinnie?

I'm waiting for you to get into your walking shoes.

But it's only 7:00 in the morning. We don't go walking until this afternoon.

Are you kidding, boss? It's going to be 90 degrees this afternoon. I'm not going out in that heat.

But we always go out in the afternoon. We've been doing it that way for almost nine years.

That's hardly any reason for doing it that way today. Today is different.

I don't know what's so different about it. Just because it's going to be warm doesn't mean we have to change the way we've always done things.

I'm telling you, boss, sometimes you amaze me with your inability to understand things.

So, why should we change?

You see, boss, things are different with us dogs. We're built differently than you, and the heat bothers us more than it does you. You may not understand that, but I do, and I have enough sense to stay in when it gets too warm. You wouldn't want me to have a heat stroke, would you?

Well, all right, if you put it that way. I'll go up and put on my walking shoes and we'll go for our walk this morning. But then what are we going to do this afternoon?

We'll cross that bridge when we get to it, boss. Boy, you sure worry a lot!

Okay, Vinnie. I'm ready. Let's go.

I'm right here, boss. Leash me up and let's hit the dusty trail.

You've been watching too much TV, Vinnie. You're beginning to sound like one of those old Westerns. But hey, it's really pleasant out here. That cool morning air feels good.

See there, boss, the change wasn't so bad after all.

No, as a matter of fact, in some ways it's better than the afternoon. Now we have the whole day ahead of us, and we get to enjoy the best time of the day out here hiking through the park.

Nice going, boss. You're doing a good job adapting to the changes. I know it's hard for you, but we dogs have always known how necessary it is to adapt to change. It's the only way we've been able to survive these many years. Why just think of where we would be if we hadn't learned how to get along with you people. I'd still be chasing rabbits instead of cars and busses.

Don't get a big head about that, Vinnie. I'd say you still have some learning to do.

REFLECTION:

How good am I at accepting change?
What changes do I have trouble with?
Are there changes I still have to deal with?

CAT SKILL

Rash judgment is a sin many of us are guilty of committing. It is so easy to place people in the pigeon hole we have created for them in our minds. We pre-judge others based on their nationality, their skin, the way they cut their hair, and kind of clothes they wear. Once we get past our pre-conceived ideas, we discover a person who is much more lovable than we would have thought.

What would you think of adopting a cat, Vinnie?

Why would you ever do something like that, boss? Is there anything cats are good for?

I'm sure they must be good for something, Vinnie. After all, God created them, and God doesn't create junk.

I guess you're right, boss, but why do you think God created cats? Can you take them for walks?

Not, long ones like you and I take.

Can they protect you from intruders, like I do?

Not very well.

Can they play catch with you?

No.

I rest my case. Cats aren't much good for anything.

Now wait just a minute, Vinnie. You're overlooking some of the things cats can do.

Like what?

For one thing, they're good at catching mice. When's the last time you brought me a mouse?

I'm not much interested in mice. What else is a cat good for? I can't imagine putting up with a cat just to get an occasional mouse.

Well, I read of a cat named Winnie, who helped save her family's lives.

No kidding? How did that happen?

It was in New Castle, Indiana. A gasoline powered water pump in the basement was emitting carbon monoxide and filling the house.

What did Winnie do?

She jumped up on the bed and starting meowing wildly, like she was trying to scream at them.

Did they get up?

Fortunately they did and they called 9-1-1. When the paramedics arrived, they found their fourteen year old son lying unconscious on the floor by his bedroom.

Was everyone all right?

Yes, they were taken to the hospital and treated for carbon monoxide poisoning, and they all recovered. But they credit Winnie, the cat, with saving their lives.

Wow! That's something. You say that cat's name was Winnie?

Yes.

Hmmm, it sounds a lot like Vinnie. I wonder if she might be a distant relative.

Now that would be something—a dog with a cat for a relative.

I guess you're right, boss, but I must confess, I wouldn't have given a cat that much credit. I guess you never know a person as well as you think you do. I'll have to rethink that adoption idea.

REFLECTION:

What causes me to prejudge others?

How can I get to know others better?

How should I react to people who express their prejudices to me?

"F" IS FOR FAITHFUL

Fidelity is an element of our faith, which asks not only that we accept the teachings of Jesus and the Church, but also that we remain faithful to those teachings. Sometimes we find the values and ways of the world more attractive or we are tempted to abandon our faith as a result of new scientific findings or new philosophies. The sins of the Church and the failure of its leaders can also weaken our faith. When all is said and done, we are left with the question of Peter: "Lord to whom shall we go?"

Hey, boss, look at all those dogs over there. What are they doing?

That's the dog park, Vinnie. People take their dogs there so they can run around and play with each other.

No kidding? Let's take a look.

Now remember to be nice while you're in there, Vinnie. There are a lot of other dogs here you've never met, so don't be overly friendly. Just take your time and allow the other dogs to get to know you before you go getting all crazy with them. Vinnie, come back, I wasn't through telling you how to behave.

This place is really special, boss. I've never seen so many dogs: big ones, little ones; young and old. The little ones are really something, they act like they own the place. Look at that little guy over there, running around telling all the others what to do.

That's part of what I wanted to tell you, Vinnie, but you ran off so fast, I didn't have a chance.

Sorry, boss, I got carried away.

Well, go on now and enjoy yourself. I'll call you when it's time to go.

Okay, boss. I'll listen for you.

Vinnie! ...Vinnie!... Vinnie!...

Didn't you hear me calling for you, Vinnie?

I heard you, boss, but I was having so much fun, I thought I would just stay here a little longer with my new friends.

That sure was embarrassing, Vinnie. All those other dog bosses were watching me and listening to me yelling as loud as I could. I tried every trick I knew, and you just paid no attention. I had to walk all the way to the other end of this park to get you.

Sometimes I wonder about you, Vinnie. They say that so many dogs are called Fido because that's the Latin word for fidelity. You're supposed to be faithful to me, but here you are running after all these new friends of yours and paying no attention to me.

Well, you've got to admit, boss, that these guys speak my language and they run a whole lost faster than you. And sometimes I don't really understand the things you say.

Well, Vinnie, do you want to go home with me, or stay here with your friends?

Let's go, boss. These others won't care for me the way you do. Let's face it. You're the only game in town.

REFLECTION:

What causes me to question my faith?
How do I deal with these doubts?
What can I do to strengthen my faith?

You're the only game in town

THOSE WERE THE DAYS

Seeing children and young people, and watching them experience life is a constant reminder to older people that their lives are not what they once were. At times, this can lead to sadness and yearning "for the days that are no more." It is in such times that we ask to be able to give thanks for the memories we have of the days when we were young. We also ask for the grace to enjoy the blessings of the present. All of life, from birth to death, is a blessing and a promise of even better days to come.

Hey, Vinnie, you've got a visitor.
I do? Who is it?

Her name is Meadow, and she's quite a good looking young lass. Come and see her.

Oh my! She is nice looking, isn't she? Where did she come from?

She was rescued by one of our families, and they wanted you to meet her.

It looks like she might be a distant relative. She has some of the same Golden Retriever blood as I do, except that she really is golden. I think I'm going to enjoy getting to know her better. Tell her to wait a second, while I go to get us something to chase after.

I see you've brought her your favorite toy puppy. That was very kind of you.

I thought I might make a good impression on her with this one. I know how women love these little pups.

Well, why don't you invite Meadow to go outside and play in the courtyard with you? I think she might enjoy that, and so would I.

C'mon Meadow, follow me, I'll show you where I play. Whoa! Meadow. I said follow me. You're already way ahead of me. Wait up, I'll show you how to chase after this thing.

I'm telling you, boss, this Meadow is really quick. I'm having trouble keeping up with her. How old is she anyway?

I'd say she's about two years old.

That explains it. I didn't realize how I've slowed down these past few years. Meadow reminds me of when I was young. I was fast like Meadow then, wasn't I, boss?

Oh yes, you surely were. When you were younger, I had trouble keeping up with you, just as you are having trouble keeping up with Meadow now.

Those were the days, weren't they boss? It's been nearly six years. I can remember the time when I could run like the wind and never grow tired. I don't know where the time went.

They were good days, Vinnie. You and I are both getting older, and if makes you feel any better; I don't run as fast either.

Well, boss, let's not worry about it. That was then and this is now. You and I may have lost a step, but look how we've grown to appreciate the goodness of the life we have. That's something to be thankful for, and all the wonderful memories we have. Thank God we still have a memory. By the way, where's what's her name?

REFLECTION:

Looking back, what are the good memories I cherish?

Am I growing older gracefully and not becoming bitter or angry?

Am I able to share the benefits of age with those younger and still learning?

WHAT IS OF VALUE

We are pretty good at collecting toys of all sorts. At the time they seem really important to us, but as time goes on, we begin to lose interest in them. There are few possessions that can bring us lasting pleasure. The accumulation of possessions can be a symptom of a spiritual disorder. If we continually look to having more things to fill the emptiness in our lives, we can get so caught up in them that there is no time or place left for God. As Pascal noted, only God can fill the emptiness we experience. In the words of the old spiritual: "You may have all this world, give me Jesus."

Vinnie! Look at this house. It's a mess.

What's wrong with it, boss? It looks all right to me.

Well just look, Vinnie. Your toys are all over the place. Why don't you keep your toys in your box until you're ready to play with them?

Actually, boss, I have a reason for taking them all out of the box.

What's the reason?

You see, I'm in the process of evaluating them. Over the years I've collected so many toys, that now I have to begin sorting them out to decide which ones to keep and which ones to get rid of.

Is it necessary to get rid of any? Why can't you just keep all of them?

Because the box is full, boss, and I don't have room for any more.

What makes you think you're going to need room for more toys? It seems to me you already have more than you need.

That's true, boss, but Christmas is coming, and I'm sure there will be more toys to add to my collection. I need to make room for them.

So, which ones are you thinking of discarding?

Well, some of them are getting pretty old and starting to leak cotton. I know how you yell at me when that happens, so I thought I might throw them out.

You won't get any argument from me on that one.

I didn't think I would.

Are there any others you plan to throw out?

Actually, boss, there are very few here that satisfy me anymore. Some of them are not too bad, like the ones that make a lot of noise, but I'm getting a little tired of them.

So what are you going to do?

I'm just going to wait for the perfect toy to come along.

And how will you know it when it comes?

That won't be hard, boss, I've been dreaming of it for a long time. It's loud and really wiggly, so when I shake it, I can feel it smacking me on the side of my head. And of course, it's durable, so it will last a long time, maybe forever.

That sounds like a really great toy, Vinnie. Do you think they make such a toy?

I'm sure they do, boss, and if it comes this Christmas, I've got room for it in my box.

REFLECTION:

Is shopping a means of filling up the empty moments in my life?

Are there things I could more usefully share with those who have less than I do?

Does my consumption of material things contribute to problems like global warming, unjust labor practices, or unwillingness to share my wealth with others?

Am I prepared to welcome the really perfect gift that comes to me each Christmas?

ALL SHE HAD TO GIVE

In a world where we have so much, there is a danger in thinking that we can please others and earn their love with gifts and other material things. Parents are tempted to equate love for their children by purchasing the latest in fashionable clothes and the most expensive shoes. Children are conditioned in a world of advertised consumerism to think they need all these things to be happy. They may want them, but they don't need them. They need love. If love is offered, the temporary disappointment of not having the latest toy will soon be forgotten.

Uh-oh, boss. Look at all those children up ahead.
Yes, Vinnie, it looks like Portage Path School is just letting out.

I'd better brace myself, I know what's coming. They're going to be hugging me and telling me how cute I am.

Well, Vinnie, that's the price you pay for being such a friendly dog. Look how anxious that little girl is to see you.

She sure is little, boss. She's not much taller than I am.

No she isn't, and from the way she's dressed, it doesn't look like she has a whole lot of money. I'll bet her mother has to work hard just to take care of her.

Oh, isn't he cute. Can I pet him?

Oh boy, here we go, boss, this is so embarrassing.

How old is he?

Gosh, boss, she's getting rather personal, don't you think?

He's about eight years old.

You don't have to tell her everything, boss.

Ha-ha, he's older than you are.

Did you hear what that kid said, boss? He told her I was older than she is. What a revoltin' development this is turning out to be.

There's no getting around it, Vinnie, you are getting older.

I guess so, but there's no need to make a fuss over it.

Oh no, here it comes, I'm going to get one of those bear hugs from that little girl. They always grab me right around the neck. Now watch, boss, she's going to put her head on my neck and tell me how much she likes me. Ohhh boy, being a church dog sure is demanding!

You should be happy, Vinnie, you're making her feel very good. Who knows, maybe she never had a dog of her own.

Oh, I don't really mind doing it, boss, especially for someone like this little girl. As you say, she probably doesn't have too much and if I can bring a little joy into her life, it's worth it.

Since, you've been so good about it, Vinnie, remind me to give you a treat when we get home. After all, you should get rewarded for the good things you do.

That would be nice, boss, and I'd appreciate one of those good biscuits, but you really don't have to. That little girl didn't have much, but she gave me something better than a treat. She gave me her love.

Good for you, Vinnie. You're growing wise as you grow older. Is that your tail I see wagging?

REFLECTION:

How does advertising and peer pressure shape the way I think about the importance of things?

What are some of the gifts I can offer, which cost only my time and attention?

How can we help our children to resist the messages they receive about material possessions and their importance?

If I can bring a little joy into her life it's worth it

UNLEASHED

Someone once said that we live in an "antinomian age", an age in which there are no laws or rules. In many ways that is true, but we also recognize the need for guidelines if society is to function properly. This is also true concerning the Church. Sometimes we grow impatient with the rules we need to observe, but they are for the common good and protect all of us from harm.

Hey, Vinnie, you ready to take a walk?

Is the Pope Catholic, boss?

Do I have to wear that thing, boss? I really don't like it. Can't we go to the cemetery? That's my favorite place, because I don't have to wear that darn leash there.

Not today, Vinnie, we're going to walk through the neighborhood. Maybe you'll see some of your old friends.

That's good, but I don't know why I have to wear that silly leash. I'm not going to attack anybody. You know that.

Yes, I know, Vinnie, but this leash is for your protection, not theirs

Why do you say that, boss? I don't see how that little thing is going to do me much good.

You know how you like to attack buses and trucks and cars with other dogs in them.

I can't help that. I just can't control myself.

That's why you need a leash. You can't control yourself, so you need this leash to control you. You may not know it, but if you get into a fight with a bus or a truck or a car, you're going to lose. You're not as strong as you think you are.

I guess you're right about that, boss. The few times I've wrestled with a car, I've lost big time.

Sometimes it doesn't seem fair, boss. I never see you wearing a leash. Don't you ever need one?

Of course I do, Vinnie, we all need one.

I've never seen your leash, boss.

That's because it's an invisible leash, but it's still very real.

No kidding, boss, how does it work?

Well, Vinnie, my leash is written in my heart. It's all the rules and laws I am expected to keep. They keep me from doing dumb things to myself or others.

Wow, does everybody have on of these leashes?

They do, Vinnie, but sometimes they don't pay any attention to it, or they think they can get along without it.

What happens then, boss?

Then they get into trouble or they get others into trouble. Sometimes they even hurt themselves or others, just like you, when you walk without a leash.

I guess I'd better wear my leash then.

Yes, at least until you get to the cemetery. Then you won't need it.

REFLECTION:

Do I appreciate the importance of abiding by the law?

Do I sometimes make exceptions for myself?

What is the spiritual value of bending to the will of another?

THE BEST GIFT

Ours is very definitely a consumerist society. We have made an art of shopping, and the only problem we have is the problem of over-choice. Which discount store will I patronize? What brand of dishwashing soap will I buy? These are decisions which remind us of how we depend on the purchase of goods to fill up our lives. Just as we tend to go shopping whenever there is something missing in our lives, hoping that our latest acquisition will fill the emptiness we feel, we also find ourselves thinking that we can fulfill our responsibilities to others through a thoughtful purchase. With friends, this may simply be a waste of time and money; with family and children it can be disastrous. The greatest gift we can give is the gift of our time, our attention, our love.

Hey, boss, what do you say we go out and do a little shopping?

Shopping? Are you kidding? You've never done any shopping in your life.

Yeah, I know, but I thought it would be nice to get a little gift for some of those people who have been so good to me.

Do you have any idea of what you want to get for them?

Yes, I've been giving it a lot of thought, and I think I know what they would like.

Tell me about it.

Well, first of all I would like to get something for all those people who remember to bring me treats.

What are you going to get for them?

I thought they might like an edible gift in return, so I'm going to dig up some of my old bones. They're nicely aged by now, and I think they would make a wonderful gift for someone who appreciates fine dining.

I'll withhold comment on that. What else do you have in mind?

I have to get something for all those who bring me toys to chew on. That's a little more difficult, since I've never had to shop for toys.

Have you come up with any ideas?

As a matter of fact, I have. I saw a really neat rubber chicken sticking out of someone's car one day and I immediately knew it would make a great gift for someone who likes things to chew on. I thought it was rather attractive and I think you could chew on it for a long time without destroying it. A rubber chicken would be a great addition to anyone's toy collection.

Vinnie, I appreciate your concern, and I'm proud of you for thinking of others, but I think you need a little advice when it comes to picking out gifts for people.

You don't think my gifts would be appreciated?

I'm sure they would be appreciated, but I'm not sure they would be appropriate.

So, what would you suggest?

I would suggest that you continue to give them what they want from you.

What's that?

Just be you. Show them how happy you are to see them, cheer them up with your bright eyes and wagging tail. Put your chin on their lap, look up longingly at them, and let them rub their fingers through your coat. That's what people want.

That's all?

That's everything. That's giving them a part of you.

REFLECTION:

Do I go shopping to relieve my boredom?

How much would I buy if I bought only the things I really need?

Am I as generous with my time and attention as I should be?

What is the one gift I have within me that I can share with others?

TO GO OR NOT TO GO

Anyone interested in growing their spiritual life is advised to have a spiritual director. Spiritual directors are people who can advise us concerning the decisions we make which will affect our relationship with God. No one should presume to be their own spiritual guide. Spiritual directors can sometimes be one person who has our trust, or it can be a group with whom we meet and discuss spiritual matters. We are not bound to follow the advice of others, but often it is the wise thing to do.

Are you ready to go out for a walk, Vinnie?

Are you crazy, boss? Do you know how cold it is out there?

According to this thermometer it's up to 7 degrees above zero. That's not so bad.

I suppose it isn't, boss. I'll go with you, but you have to promise me one thing.

What's that?

That you'll stay off the sidewalks with a lot of salt on them. That salt may be all right for you, but remember, I don't have any shoes and that salt can be pretty hard on my feet.

I think I can manage to avoid the salt, Vinnie. There are plenty of places where there is not salt.

OK, boss, get your coat on and let's give it a go.

This isn't so bad, is it Vinnie? Actually, it feels rather refreshing.

No it isn't as bad as I thought it might be. This coat of mine is made for weather like this. I'm doing better than I do on those really hot days of summer. That's when my coat can become a hazard. I rather like the cold.

Well, I think we've gone about a mile out, Vinnie. Maybe we ought to turn back, just in case the trip home is colder than the trip out.

That's fine with me, boss. I've gone far enough and there isn't much to hunt for on these sidewalks. They've been picked clean by someone.

Let's just circle around then and head for home.

Whoa, boss! You didn't tell me about this wind. Wow, this is really something. I can hardly catch my breath.

Me too, Vinnie, and my eyes are watering from the cold. It feels like it's about 20 below out here now.

Did you check the wind chill before we left home, boss?

Yes, it was 20 below.

For heaven's sake, boss why didn't you say so? We shouldn't be out here in this kind of weather.

I think you're right, Vinnie. I did hear them say on the radio that we shouldn't go out on days like this, but I thought you and I could handle it.

Well, think again, boss. This is insane. How much farther do we have?

Not much, Vinnie, about another mile. We'll make it. Just cover your mouth.

Very funny, boss. Which paw do you suggest I use? Hey boss, do me a favor. The next time someone tells you not to do something, why not listen to them?

Reflection:

1. To whom do I go for spiritual advice?
2. In what ways do I learn from others?
3. Does anyone consider me their spiritual advisor?

Are you ready to go out for a walk?

JUNK FOOD

Following God's ways can only make us better persons, but we often prefer to choose our own ways, and that leads us into temptation and often sin. The delights of this world can be good and wholesome, but there is always that temptation to taste the forbidden fruit, which can appear so inviting and irresistible. Forbidden fruit can take the form of that which is outright wrong, such as stealing or cheating, but more often it appears as simply overindulging in that which of itself is good, such as television or shopping.

Hey, Vinnie, what happened to the butter?
Butter?

Yes. There was a whole stick of butter on the table just now.

Oh, that butter.

Yes, that butter. What happened to it?

I cannot tell a lie, boss, I ate it.

You what? Vinnie! How many times have I told you not to take food from the table? You mean you ate that whole stick of butter?

Well, I didn't see any reason for leaving any of it there. I know you would have thrown it out.

But Vinnie, don't you know that people food, especially butter, isn't good for you? The next time we go to your doctor, we'll have to have your cholesterol checked.

It may not be good for me, but it sure tasted good; better than that nasty table spread you use.

You mean you've eaten that too?

Oops. I guess I'd better keep my mouth shut.

I thought you dogs had more sense than we humans. I thought you knew what was good for you and not eat anything that was going to hurt you.

Well, that's partially true, boss, but sometimes our appetite gets in the way of our good sense. That's when we get into trouble.

You know, Vinnie, sometimes you help me understand God a little better

What do you mean, boss?

Well, just like I try to give you good food to keep you healthy and out of trouble, God gives us good food to keep us healthy and make us better. At times, though, we prefer to eat the food that isn't good for us. We think our way of eating and finding pleasure is better than what God offers us. When we do that we get into trouble and forget to accept the food our Father provides.

That does sound a lot like me, boss.

Yes, it does. So now I know how God must feel when we refuse the food he gives us and prefer to eat the food we think will make us happy. I don't think God is angry so much, he is just sad to think that we could have done so much better by eating his heavenly food .

Gosh, boss, when you put it that way, I feel bad. I'm sorry about the butter. Is there anything I can do to make it better?

Well, yes, as a matter of fact there is, Vinnie. How about leaving my food alone and sticking to your own food?

It sounds tough, boss, but I'll give it the old college try.

REFLECTION:

Is there somebody I can discuss my spiritual growth with?

Do I need a spiritual director with whom I can meet regularly?

What are some of the things I would discuss with a spiritual director?

GETTING ALONG

We all have difficulty getting along with people who are different from us. This can lead to problems from neighborhood arguments to world wars. In our country there is a long history of racism, which has caused the sin of segregation and social injustice. Failing to appreciate the differences we have and the variety of gifts present in other races and cultures harms not only those we isolate, but ourselves as well. We are the poorer for it.

That sure was nice of Bridget to invite us to the opening of the towpath trail extension, boss.

Yes, it was, Vinnie, but you have a funny way of showing your appreciation. I mean, did you have to bark so loudly at that mule.

I was excited, boss. That's the first time I ever saw one of those things.

Yes, but it was very embarrassing, Vinnie. There were a lot of people there. They were all dressed up and prepared for a special presentation to open the new extension, and there you were barking so loudly that everybody was wondering what was happening.

It was very clear what was happening, boss. That mule was prancing around like he owned the place. I just needed to let him know that I was there too.

But he was there for a special reason, Vinnie. He was invited to remind people about the canal days, when mules like him used to tow the boats along the towpath we walk on.

No kidding, boss. If I had known that I might have behaved a little differently. I thought he was just another mule. You know, the kind "with long funny ears that kicks up at anything he hears. His back is brawny but his brain is weak. He's just plain stupid with a stubborn streak."

All right, Bing, but the fact is that you and I were clearly invited to walk a little distance from the mule. I mean, we all but got thrown out.

Like, I said, boss, if I had known why that mule was there, I might have behaved a little better.

You see that's the point, Vinnie. You should never judge an individual, even a mule, by the way they look. Everybody has a place in our world and every person is special. You need to learn how to look beyond the floppy ears and the stubborn streak. and appreciate the gifts each one has.

I'll try to remember that, boss. It's something I have trouble with.

Look at it this way, Vinnie. Your ears are pretty floppy too, and you wouldn't want others to judge you by your ears.

You're right about that, boss. But aside from all that, I did enjoy our walk along the new extension, even if we had to do it alone. It's very interesting and I think a lot of people are going to enjoy it.

I'm sure they will, Vinnie. I enjoyed seeing the remains of the locks and I thought of our former parishioners who worked so hard to help build all of that. It was like walking back in time. I also liked the new covered bridges. They're really nice.

Yes they are, boss.

How about you, Vinnie, what did you like best?

The mule.

The mule? After the way you carried on?

Yes, he kind of reminded me of myself.

He did?

You know, he was someone special—like me.

REFLECTION:

Do I harbor prejudices against others?

What am I doing to overcome these feelings?

What are the gifts other races and cultures can share with me?

RIGHT ON THE MONET

"This people has eyes to see, but does not see; ears to hear but does not hear." We all have the ability to develop our senses so that they become more alert to the impressions they receive. Sensory overload is an ever present danger in an age so tuned in. Our senses are constantly bombarded with sights and sounds, to the point we learn to tune out in order to find peace. Learning to appreciate the difference between noise and sound, seeing and perceiving is necessary for enjoying the beauty that surrounds us.

Good evening, boss. Did you have a nice day off?

Yes, I did, Vinnie. I went to the Cleveland Museum of Art to visit the Monet exhibit.

What's that?

It's a collection of paintings by the French Impressionist artist, Claude Monet.

I never heard of him.

I didn't think you had, Vinnie. That's something we haven't talked about very much.

What's so special about this Monet guy?

Well, besides being the originator of Impressionism, I like the cheerfulness of his painting. He uses wonderful colors and really makes one feel like he's right in the middle of the scene he's portrayed. It's as if you can feel the wind blowing and the warm sun shining on your face. You can almost smell the flowers and the sea mist on your face.

That does sound nice, boss. Did you smell anything worth eating?

No, it isn't that real, Vinnie. It just feels real.

I suppose it is like looking at one of those pictures we see on television. If this Monet were living today, he'd probably be a photographer, don't you think?

Oh no, not at all. Painting is all together different from taking a picture.

No kidding? How so?

Well a painter not only shows you a picture of what he sees, he can also tell you how he feels about what he sees. He portrays more than a beautiful scene; he portrays how he experiences that scene.

Sounds pretty tricky to me. How does he do that?

First of all he learns the technique. He learns how to paint.

I think I understand that. It's like the special technique I have for taking doughnuts from a person's hand without their ever knowing it—it's called the soft mouth technique, and only a few dogs have it.

Yes, something like that, Vinnie. But besides technique, a painter also has to have to a special eye which allows him to see things differently than you or I might see them. It's almost as if he can see into the very essence of a subject and put it on a canvas.

That sounds like a really special gift, boss. I can't even see colors that well, much less an essence.

I guess that's true, Vinnie, but you make up for it with your nose.

I never thought of that, boss. Just think, I have the nose of an artist.

I wouldn't have put it that way, Vinnie, but in a way, I guess you're right.

Well, I'm glad you enjoyed yourself today, boss. You know, I sometimes think you people don't appreciate what is right in front of your eyes. Maybe a little Monet will help.

REFLECTION:

Do I take the time to look at the beauty that surrounds me; to listen to the music that soothes me?

How can I develop my sensibility to the arts?

How can an appreciation of the arts contribute to my prayer?

I have the nose of an artist

LOST AND FOUND

We may not know it, but we all have a homing device built into us, something that constantly reminds us of home. When we get into trouble and don't know where to turn, something tells us there is a power outside of us that points to the One who has the answer to our problem. When we examine the beauty and the mystery of our creation, we sense there must be a reason for all this to be the way it is. It can't be mere chance. Try as we might to overlook this, we can't rid ourselves of this homing device. It points us in the right direction and it is imbedded in our souls.

What's that you're reading, boss?

I'm reading about Mickey.

Who's Mickey?

Mickey's a Boston Terrier.

What's so interesting about him?

Mickey was lost, and now he has been found and is back home with his family.

Doesn't sound all that interesting to me.

Ordinarily it wouldn't be. But listen to this. Mickey disappeared four years ago.

That's a long time to be gone. What happened, did he get mad at his boss and run away?

Nobody knows, but that isn't all.

There's more?

Yes. Mickey was living in Kansas City when he disappeared from his backyard, and guess where they found him.

In the front yard?

No! They found him 1,100 miles away in Billings, Montana.

That is interesting. I wonder how he got there.

So is everybody else.

Do you think Mickey walked all the way to Montana?

I doubt it, boss. Boston Terriers aren't very big, and that would be a pretty long walk for a little dog. Maybe he hitched a ride or jumped a train.

Could be. At any rate, he ended up a long way from home.

How did the people in Montana know who was Mickey's boss.

That's also interesting. Mickey's boss was very smart and planted a microchip on Mickey which identified who he belonged to.

Sounds to me like Mickey may have had a bit of wanderlust in him, if his boss had to do that.

Would you like one of those microchips?

I don't need one, boss. I'm not one to stray too far, and besides, I've got my own microchip.

You do?

Oh my, yes. It's firmly planted in my mind. If for some strange reason I should stray and get lost, I would never forget where I came from and who it was that saved me.

We all need one of those microchips, Vinnie.

REFLECTION:

What are the things that point my mind to God?
Does a day go by that I don't think of God?
Do I take time in those moments to say a little prayer of praise or thanksgiving?

SEMPER FIDELIS

God made a woman to be a companion for the man, and ever since we humans have sought companionship. Marriage is the ordinary way in which we form a companionship for life. Marriage not only gives us the support and help we need from another, but the relationship of man and women in marriage helps to perfect the person we already are. Fidelity in marriage can be difficult, but in working out life's problems, we learn more about ourselves and the changes we need to make. Not all are called to marriage, but all are in need of good and faithful friends.

Are you going away again, boss?

I was supposed to go on retreat this week, Vinnie, but it was cancelled, so I'll be staying home.

That's good, boss. I don't like it when you go away.

I know that, Vinnie, but I don't know what to do about it. I have to go away sometimes.

I've been thinking, boss. Maybe I ought to get a companion dog. If I had a companion dog, I wouldn't mind your going away as much.

What would you do with a companion dog, Vinnie? You'd just bark at it the way you do other dogs.

Oh, no, boss. One doesn't bark at a companion dog. I would treat it with the utmost kindness and generosity. After all, a companion dog isn't like any other dog.

Is that right, Vinnie? And just how would such a dog be any different from the others.

Well, for one thing it would have to be a dog I could get along with. A dog that enjoyed doing the kinds of things I like to do. You know, like chasing after balls, and toys and busses.

That kind of dog may be hard to find, Vinnie.

Maybe so, boss, but I know there's a dog out there for me. I just have to be patient.

I'm sure you're right about that, Vinnie, but I wouldn't want your companion dog to be exactly like you.

Why not, boss? Don't you like me the way I am?

Sure I do, Vinnie, but a good companion dog would perhaps add to the good dog you already are. Your companion dog may be able to do a better job of getting food from difficult places.

You've got something there, boss. Maybe someone just a little smaller than I am. We could work together as a team. I could do some things my companion couldn't, and vice versa.

Now you've got it, Vinnie.

Yes, boss, and on top of that, my companion dog would be just that—a companion. Someone I could take walks with and go hunting with. You know, we dogs are just like you in that respect. We need to be with others.

You're right, Vinnie. But having a companion dog means you would probably have to give up your attachment to me. Are you prepared to do that?

Now, boss, you know better than to ask a question like that. That's the dog's code of honor. We are always faithful up to the end, no matter what. Hey, c'mon boss, where's your sense of humor? I was just kidding about that companion dog thing. C'mon, let's go for our walk.

REFLECTION:

How grateful am I for the good friends I have, especially my spouse?

Do I return the gift of friendship the way I should?

Do I do all I can to protect my marriage?

If I am not married, do I have other appropriate ways of meeting my need for companionship?

WHO ONLY STAND
AND WAIT

Contrary to the traditional American ideology, the fact is that not all are created equal. St. Thomas used a rather earthy example to indicate this truth. He said that if you wanted someone to evaluate the quality of a particular vintage, you would choose the person with the best taster. Only a true connoisseur can judge the character of wine, and not all have that inborn ability. Once we can accept that we may not have the gifts and talents of others, we can begin to look for the particular talents we do possess, then we can set out to serve in the best way we can.

Where are you going, boss?
I'm going over to the hospital to visit someone who is sick.

Can I come?

I don't think so, Vinnie. You have to become a member of the Doggie Brigade to do that.

What's a Doggie Brigade?

Members of the Doggie Brigade get a special uniform to wear and they are permitted to visit patients and cheer them up.

That sounds simple enough. I can do that.

Yes, there's no doubt you could cheer others, you do that all the time, but there's more to it than that. You have to pass a test to qualify as a member of the Doggie Brigade.

No kidding? What would I have to do to pass the test?

First you have to be able to sit, lie down, walk on a leash, and come when you are called.

I think I could get that part pretty well. I don't always come when called, but if I thought it was important enough, I probably would. What else?

You have to allow others to pet you without becoming defensive or aggressive.

That's easy. I love it when people pet me. What's next?

You have to demonstrate that you are people oriented.

That's a no brainer. Just show me a person, and I'm Joe Friendly. Give me a hard one.

OK. You can't react to sudden sounds or movements from others.

That could be a problem. I'm a little jittery in such circumstances, but not enough to keep me from doing important work. C'mon, give me a really hard one.

All right, how about this? You have to avoid aggressive or exuberant behavior when in the presence of other dogs.

Uh-oh! I think I've met my Waterloo. There's no way I can control myself around other dogs. I just get too excited.

Yes, I know that, Vinnie. That's why I've never entered you as a candidate for the Doggie Brigade. I knew you would feel badly, if you failed the test.

Yes, I would have, boss. I pride myself on being able to do things like that, and it would have been disappointing to know that I am not capable of helping the sick, especially sick children.

Well, Vinnie, then you've learned an important lesson. There are some things we would like to do, but God hasn't given us the gifts to do them.

Right, boss. But I'll still do the things I can do well, and use the gifts I have in other ways. Like you've told me: "They also serve who only stand and wait."

REFLECTION:

Do I judge myself against those who are more gifted than I?

What are the talents I have been given?

How can I use my talents in a way that helps others?

I'll still do the things I can do well

LIFT UP YOUR EYES

There is a close relationship between trust and faith. In some cases they are synonymous. If we really believe in the goodness of God, we will place our trust in him. When we worry about what we are to eat and what we are to wear, it is a sign that we may not believe as firmly as we thought. We tend to want to hedge our belief by storing up for the times we may not have enough. The goodness God has shown in the past should convince us that God will not abandon us in time of need.

Hey, Vinnie, why do you keep doing that?
Doing what, boss?

We're walking along at a nice brisk pace and all of a sudden you stop and smell something you see on the ground. Why do you do that?

I'm just checking, boss. It may be food.

But, Vinnie, you shouldn't be eating that stuff. You never know what it is and how old it might be. Most of what you find on the ground isn't good for you anyway.

I know, boss, but it sure tastes good. I love those French fries and chicken bones.

Yes, Vinnie, but just because they taste good, that doesn't make them good for you. You need to eat healthier food. Oops, there you go again. What is it this time?

That wrapper there, boss, I thought it might have a few chips left in it.

To watch you go after food, Vinnie, you'd think you were starving.

No, you give me plenty of food, boss, and it's good for me, but sometimes the stuff out here looks so attractive.

I guess you're a lot like people, Vinnie.

You mean people stop and smell things too?

No, of course not, but they keep searching for things they like and things that look attractive. You go after chicken bones and brightly colored wrappers. People go after things like bigger homes, better neighborhoods, nicer furniture, and newer cars. A lot of things like that which they think will make them happier. But once they have them, they find they don't really satisfy their needs and sometimes they're not even good for them.

You're right, boss. I need to stop looking at the ground all the time and start looking up.

We all need to learn that, Vinnie. I guess you and I have more in common than we thought. We can't seem to take our eyes off the things of the earth.

Maybe that's what the prophet meant, boss, when he said "Lift up your eyes and see."

Good thinking, Vinnie. You know you really don't need to worry about getting the food you need. That's what I'm here for.

I know that, boss. And your food is really the best there is, but sometimes I'm afraid I may not have enough, so I keep looking for more.

That's not going to happen, Vinnie. You should know by now that I always provide for you, even when it seems your bowl is getting empty.

I'm going to work on that, boss. It's just that sometimes I get to thinking the food I find down on the ground is better. I need to learn to live on the food you supply.

Vinnie! Don't even think of picking up that old cookie.

REFLECTION:

Do I really believe that God will provide what is best for me?

Am I willing to forfeit my own thoughts about what is good and accept God's will?

In what areas am I most inclined to provide for myself, rather than trust God?

REAL FOOD

In a consumer society like ours, there are many items we can purchase to fill up the emptiness in our lives, but none of them is capable of filling what the philosopher Blaise Pascal called "a God-shaped vacuum." What delights us and satisfies a temporary need is often more attractive than the gifts God offers, and we sometimes choose to spend our time and our treasure in pursuing that which is only a shadow. Searching for the truth that will bring what we are looking for is a worthwhile effort, and will eventually lead us to the bread that satisfies.

Hey, Vinnie, do you want to go shopping?

What are we shopping for, boss?

We need to get you some more dog food.

Here's my leash, boss, what are we waiting for?

Come on. I'll let you help pick out the food you want.

This is a great store, boss. Look everything in here is for dogs.

Not, exactly, Vinnie, they also have things for cats and birds and even fish.

Well, the important stuff is for dogs. Let's take a look at what they have to offer.

How about these things, boss, I never saw so many snacks and things to chew on. Look at those bones. They look delicious. And those green things, I'll bet they're good for you.

They're supposed to freshen your breath, but I don't know if they do much good.

That's all right, boss, maybe we could get a pig ear or two.

The trouble with all these snacks, Vinnie, is that they aren't very nourishing. You can't live on just snacks. They're fun to eat, but after that you have nothing to show for it.

That's the trouble with life, boss, the fun things aren't always good for you, but they sure are tempting.

I'll grant you that, Vinnie, but too many of them can land you in trouble. It's best to stay away from them. Just listen to me; I'll help you choose what's best for you.

Look over here, boss, they've got bags of regular, everyday dog food.

That's what we're looking for, Vinnie, some food for every day that will keep you healthy and in good shape.

But there are so many to choose from, boss. How am I supposed to know which one is the best? Maybe I could have a little taste of each.

I don't think they would let you do that, Vinnie. Let's just read what is in each of them. That will help us decide which one is best for you.

I can save you the time of doing that, boss. I've already found the one I think would be best.

Sure, it's also the most expensive one, but not necessarily the best for you.

How about this, boss? It's new and much better than all the others. It promises to keep me living well and living longer—maybe forever.

If it's that good, Vinnie, you've got to have it. Grab a bag of it and we're on our way home.

REFLECTION:

Am I perhaps a compulsive shopper?

Have the things I've purchased had any lasting value?

Do I spend at least some time developing a relationship with God through quiet prayer?

NO GREATER LOVE

Once a year, we set aside a day to remember all those who have given their lives to protect our country and our freedom. Too often, we ask men and women to put their lives on the line for the love of their country, and too often lives are lost in the struggle for peace. It is good to be reminded of the sacrifices others have made for us, and Memorial Day should remind us to think more often about the insanity of war. It should urge us to work harder for real and lasting peace.

What are you looking at, Vinnie.

Oh nothing. I was just looking out this window to Market Street.

What's so interesting about Market Street?

It's not so much the street that's interesting, but I was remembering that day when I got creamed by a car out there.

I'm surprised you can remember that. You were hit pretty hard on the head by that passing car. I thought it might have impaired your memory.

No, not really. I remember lying there on the street. My eyes were open, but I couldn't move. That's when you showed up, all in a tizzy.

Yes, I must admit, I was very frightened. I thought you might be a goner.

Well, you know what I was wondering just now? I was recalling how the cars just kept speeding by us on the street and how it was really rather dangerous for us to be out there. I mean you could have been struck by a passing car yourself. Weren't you afraid of that?

To tell you the truth Vinnie, I wasn't even thinking about it. I was so upset by what had happened to you, that I wasn't thinking about my own safety.

That's pretty nice, boss. Thanks for thinking about me like that.

It's no problem, Vinnie. I'm sure if the situation were reversed, you would do the same for me.

I hope so, boss, but I might have trouble picking you up.

That's not what I meant. I mean you would do whatever you could to try to save me.

Of course, I would, boss. That's what you do when you care enough about another. You make sure they are all right, even if it costs you your life. But hey, boss, let's not try it out, OK?

I'm not planning on it, Vinnie, but you know there are many young men and women who have not been afraid to put themselves in harm's way for you and me.

Yes, I know that, boss, and I'm very appreciative of their sacrifices. It's too bad we have to do such things, but I guess that's the way the world is.

I'm afraid you're right, Vinnie. And we should never forget those who made the ultimate sacrifice of giving their lives to protect us.

That's what I like about Memorial Day, boss. It's an opportunity to pray and give thanks for those who in father Abraham's words, "gave the last full measure of devotion."

Amen to that, Vinnie. Amen to that.

REFLECTION:

Do war casualties sometimes become so frequent that we tend to become immune to them?

Are there special people in my life who have given their lives in service to their country?

What can I do to help those who serve in our military?

I was just looking out this window

SNIFFING IT OUT

Francis Thompson, the poet, referred to God as the hound of heaven. In our blindness, we may try to run from God and pursue other gods, but God will pursue us and find us. God's love for us is never ending, and we cannot hide from him, although we sometimes try. Because of God's persistent love, we learn that when we are found by God, we have also found ourselves. It was not God we were fleeing, it was our true self. "Ah, fondest, blindest, weakest, I am He Whom thou seekest ! Thou dravest love from thee, who dravest me."

Holy cow, Vinnie! Slow down. What's your hurry?

I'm after that other dog, boss.

What other dog? I don't see any other dogs around here.

That's the problem with you, boss. What you can't see, you don't believe.

Well what makes you so smart? How do you know there's another dog ahead of us?

Can't you smell it, boss? It's as plain as the nose on your face.

It may be plain to the nose on your face, but not mine.

Yes, I know, boss. I shouldn't be so short with you. I keep forgetting that you can't smell as well as I do.

Is that why you keep stopping to sniff around at nothing?

Hey, boss, it's not nothing. When I stop to sniff, it's because I've got something to sniff about.

I don't know about that. Sometimes we can be walking on the sidewalk, which is perfectly clean, and all of a sudden you stop to smell the concrete.

I don't smell concrete, boss. Concrete isn't very interesting.

Then what are you sniffing?

It could be any number of things. More often than not it's been a squirrel that crossed our path a while back.

You mean you can smell the footprints of a squirrel?

Sure, boss. That's easy. Haven't you heard of my cousin who proved just how accurately we can sniff out things?

No, what happened?

Well, people wondered if my cousin could tell one smell from another, so his boss found 11 men and had them walk directly behind him, so there was only one set of footprints, but twelve men had walked in the one set. Get it?

I think so, then what?

The twelve men walked 200 yards and dispersed, each in a different direction, and then they hid.

What did your cousin do?

He followed the one set of footprints, and when he reached the point where they had dispersed, he paused, sniffed a moment, picked up his boss's scent and followed it to his boss.

You know, that's kind of scary, Vinnie. I would have a hard time hiding from you. You can tell where I am at any moment by just following my footprints.

That's right, boss. You can't hide from me. This nose of mine will track you down.

Amazing, Vinnie. You're too sharp for me.

REFLECTION:

What other gods threaten my relationship with God or with others?

Have I been fleeing from the God who pursues me?

Am I the person I think I should be? Do I need to pay more attention to God?

NICE DOG

Love without action is empty, and nice words will never be able to substitute for charitable action. So often we read about tragedies like hunger and home-lessness, and we sympathize with their victims, but sympathy is not always enough. Responding to other needs, whether here or around the world, is the duty of all who have been blessed with an abundance of the world's blessings. St. John of the Cross tells us: "In the evening of our life we will be judged on love."

Where are we going today, boss?

Today is Friday, so that means we're going to take a stroll down Main Street.

Great. The good thing about Main Street is that there are a lot of people there. I get a lot of attention from all those folks.

Well, get your leash and let's go.

I'm coming, boss, just hold on a second.

Oh boy, here they come, boss.

Who's coming, Vinnie?

All those young ladies leaving their offices. They really like me. Watch this, boss.

"Oh, what a cutie you are."

"Isn't he sweet?"

"My, you're a honey."

See what I mean, boss. The women just can't resist me.

I also noticed that you didn't do anything to discourage them. That "poor, pitiful Pearl" routine is pretty transparent.

Yeah, but it still works, boss.

There's the bus stop just ahead, boss. Wait until you see the comments I get from the guys there.

"That's a nice looking dog."

"What kind of dog is that?"

"He looks just like my dog."

"My, what a handsome dog."

OK. You can take your nose out of the air now, Vinnie, we're past everybody.

Well, boss, I can't help it if I'm so attractive to people. That's just the way God made me.

That's true, Vinnie, and I kind of like it when people ooh and aah over you. That's why I keep saying "thank you" when you get a compliment.

I was wondering about that, boss. You thank them as if they were complimenting you.

But, to tell you the truth, boss, I really don't get all that excited about the attention paid to me. It doesn't mean that much to me.

Why is that, Vinnie? I should think you would feel good about it.

I do, up to a point, boss. But when you think about it, they're only words. In my world, boss, words don't count for much. It's action I'm looking for.

Like what, Vinnie?

Food, boss, I can't live on words. A good biscuit is worth a thousand words.

REFLECTION:

Do I take the time to become aware of the sufferings of others?

Am I generous in sharing what I have with those who have less?

TAKE A HIKE

Many people are very health conscious and aware of the need to care of their bodies. A whole industry has sprung up in response to this need. Mental health is also important. Stress is a real factor in the kind of harried lives we lead. Getting out and getting away is good advice for everybody. The same can be said of our spiritual health. We need to take time to be alone with God in prayer and meditation. A wholistic approach to life includes body, mind and spirit. The time we spend taking care of ourselves helps us take better care of others.

Come on, boss, it's time for your hike.

Why do you call it a hike, Vinnie? It's really more like a walk.

I know, but I'm trying to make it sound more attractive for you.

Do we have to go today, Vinnie, I really don't feel like taking a hike, or walk, or whatever you call it?

Now listen, boss, this is part of my job. It's my responsibility to see that you stay in shape, so you can do your work. So let's not argue about it. You're going on your hike with me now, and there's no getting around it. Now take this leash, put it on me, and let's get going.

Nag, nag, nag. You sure can be a nag sometimes.

Now, don't get upset, boss. I'm doing it for you. You need to get out and stretch, keep those legs in shape, hold on to your health, etc.

I guess you're right about that, Vinnie, but I could do all those things without leaving the house. I could get one of those walking machines and pretend I'm taking a hike right here at home.

It's not the same, boss. You also need to take care of your mental health. You're under a lot of stress, and it's important that you get out of the house. A change of scenery is like taking a vacation. When we're out walking you can forget all about your problems and just enjoy the outdoors and me.

I'd enjoy you a lot more if you didn't stop so often to smell whatever it is you smell.

That's the difference between you and me, boss. You like to look around at the trees and flowers and everything.

Don't you enjoy those things, Vinnie?

Yes, up to a point, but my vision isn't as good as yours. I see things with my nose better than with my eyes.

Is that why you enjoy taking these walks, because you get to smell new and different smells than the ones at home?

I suppose that's part of it. But I need to get away just like you. Like they say: "All work and no jog, makes Vinnie a dull dog."

I can't say I've ever heard them say that, but if you say so.

To tell you the truth, boss, there's another reason we need to take these hikes.

What's that?

Well, you see how happy people are to see me. If we didn't go on these daily jaunts, a lot of people would be disappointed. I have to get out and bring joy to others. Taking you along kills two birds with one stone.

Thanks. That makes me feel really important.

REFLECTION:

Do I set aside time in my day for exercise?

Does what I do bring enjoyment and provide for mental relaxation?

Do I set aside time for prayer and meditation?

I have to get out and bring joy to others

BE NOT AFRAID

Learning to trust in God is not always easy. When times get tough and we begin to wonder if there is any solution to our problem, we begin to doubt if God will really answer our prayers. In truth, God does not always give the answer we are looking for, but God does provide the answer which is best for us. Trusting in God means being willing to accept the answer of God: "Thy will be done." When tempted to question God's beneficent will, it is good to recall all the blessings already bestowed on us.

Where are you going, boss?
I'm going out to feed the birds.

I thought you just did that.

I did, but I didn't have enough food, so I have to give them a little more.

What do you feed those little guys? They sure seem to go through it awfully fast.

Yes, they do, don't they. I just give them bird seed. They seem to like it pretty much.

Yuck. I don't know what they see in that. You wouldn't catch me eating that stuff. It doesn't taste very good, and it gets stuck in your teeth. I don't know what those birds see in it.

Well, maybe you would if you were a bird. And, by the way, I'm glad you don't like it, or I'd be buying a lot more bird seed than I do now.

I don't see why you have to feed the birds anyway. Isn't there enough food out there for them to find their own? It seems to me they're getting off pretty easy.

I guess you're right about that, Vinnie. To tell you the truth, my motives are a bit selfish. I give them food so I can watch them and listen to their singing. They make me happy.

It doesn't take much to make you happy, boss. I wouldn't call that racket they make singing. It sounds like just a bunch of chirping to me.

Call it what you like, I still enjoy listening to it. So, enough talking. Do you want to come out with me?

No thanks. I'll just sit and watch you out the window.

Suit yourself. I'll be right back.

That didn't take long, boss. You know, those birds are crazier than I thought.

What makes you say that?

Well, they were all busily fighting each other trying to get a place at the feeder when you walked out the door, and then, when they saw you coming with more food, they all flew away. What's the matter with them?

I think they get frightened when they see me. I'm a lot bigger than they are and they probably think I might hurt them.

How could they think a thing like that? You've been feeding them every day for all these years, and by now they should know you mean them no harm. You don't see me running from my dish when you come to fill it.

That is strange, isn't it Vinnie? It seems no matter how hard I try to please them, they still don't trust me. I don't know if they ever will.

That's too bad, boss. It didn't take me long to learn that I could depend on you. I can count on you to have the food I need.

REFLECTION:

When is it hard to trust in God?
Recall the daily blessings God bestows on you.
Try to remember a time when the answer God gave
    turned out to be the right one for you.

FOOTPRINTS

It was Edmund Burke who said, "People will not look forward to posterity who never look backward to their ancestors." Oliver Cromwell, in arranging for the education of his son, said: "I would have him learn a little history." It is good to be aware to the debt we owe to those who have gone before us, near or late. The examples of faith and courage we learn from great people of the past inspire us to excel in our periods of trial. The lessons handed down to us by our family are the distillation of generations who have acquired wisdom that can be learned only through experience. We stand on the shoulders of those who have gone before us, and we step away from them at our own risk.

We've been walking in these woods for a pretty long time, boss. Don't you think we ought to head for home?

That's exactly what I've been thinking, Vinnie. As a matter of fact, I thought we were heading for home.

You mean we're lost, boss?

Yes, Vinnie, a little bit.

A little bit! What do you mean a little bit? If we're lost, we're lost. We could walk around these woods all day and never find our way out.

Now don't get nervous, Vinnie. I have confidence in you, and I know you can help us find our way home.

How am I going to do that?

With your sense of smell, just keep your nose to the ground and find the footprints of someone who has been here before. They will lead us out of here.

Good idea, boss. I can do that.

You lead; I'll follow.

I think I've picked up on something, boss.

What is it?

It's a very complex scent, a blend I believe.

What's it smell like?

There's a woody odor to it, together with a hint of nuts and, of all things, electric wires, and grass, yes, definitely grass.

Let me see what you have there.

Take a look, boss.

Just as I thought, these are squirrel tracks. They won't do us much good. Let's move on.

Got something, boss.

What is it this time?

Rather strange. There's definitely an odor of dried leaves, but also a very fine bouquet of garden plants.

Sounds like a deer to me. Not much help there. Who knows where those tracks may take us?

What we are looking for, Vinnie, is the path of a person like me who has been here before. If we can find that, we know it will take us out of the woods.

Good thinking, boss. The person ahead of us knew something we don't know. He knew where he was and where he was going.

Are you saying I don't know any of those things?

Not at all, boss, not at all. Wait! I think I've got it.

What is it?

Surefire footprint. It smells just like home. Follow me boss, I'll take you there.

REFLECTION:

Who are my heroes?

What is unique and worth holding on to in my family's history?

What do I find most admirable in my fore bearers?

TIME TO GIVE THANKS

Thanksgiving comes but once a year, however we should always have an attitude of thanks, mindful constantly of the good gifts we have received in our lives. An attitude of gratitude opens our eyes to appreciate just how many things we have to be thankful for, things which too often we take for granted. Giving thanks begins with thanking God, the source of all blessings, and then the people in our lives who make our lives especially happy and meaningful.

Do you know what today is, Vinnie?

It's Thursday, the day we walk on the towpath trail.

Yes, but this is a special Thursday. This Thursday is Thanksgiving.

Oh boy! I can't wait. Turkey, stuffing, mashed potatoes, cranberry sauce and pumpkin pie.

Now wait a minute, Vinnie. There's more to Thanksgiving than eating.

What could there be more than eating?

Just what the name implies. This is a day to give thanks for all your blessings.

Right, boss, I'll have to think about that.

You might begin by thinking of all the people who have been helpful to you.

I guess I should begin with my parents. Even though they didn't stay around very long, without them, I wouldn't be here.

I think you should go back one step further.

That's right. I should first thank God for the gift of life. My parents brought me into the world, but they couldn't have done it without God.

Next I would thank that good woman who stopped to pick me up after I had been thrown from the car and the kind person who took me in and found a home for me. And I can't forget the one who called you and told you how lucky you were to get a beautiful, intelligent, friendly dog who would bring much happiness and joy into your life, and who......

Wait a minute. Let's not get carried away. But it's good you appreciate the many people who have been helpful to you in your time of need. Sometimes we forget the people who have made our life better.

And along those lines, boss, I should thank all the people here at St. Vincent who have welcomed me so warmly: the children who are so happy to see me and the people who smile when I go to church and give me a pat on the back. I especially want to thank those who remember to bring a treat to church with them. Come to think of it, I guess I never appreciated how many people there are to thank and how important this church is to me.

That's right, Vinnie. It's the people in our lives who give us the best gift of all. They give us their love and affection.

You know, boss, there really is more to Thanksgiving than eating. But wait, boss there's one more person I ought to thank for my daily food and water... Thank you, boss.

REFLECTION:

Begin by counting the blessings you have received.
Next, focus on one blessing and reflect more carefully on how it has been a blessing.
End by offering a prayer of thanksgiving which
comes from the heart and goes to God.

There really is more to Thanksgiving than eating

HAVE A HEART

Walking the streets of our cities reveals a society much more sympathetic to the needs of those who are physically challenged. Wheelchair accessibility at all street corners has made it possible for those in motorized wheelchairs to get around almost as easily as those who are physically able. This social concern for others is an attitude we all hope to develop, and sometimes we need to be made aware of the hardships others bear, which we have been spared.

Are you ready for our walk, Vinnie?

Excuse me, boss, but did I hear you correctly? Did you say walk?

I did, Vinnie, it's that time. You know—walk time.

Have you looked out the door, boss? Do you know there's a foot of snow out there?

That shouldn't be any problem, Vinnie. You've got your winter coat on and I'm all bundled up and ready to go.

Well, it may not be a problem for you, boss, but it does present me with a bit of a problem.

Don't tell me you're afraid of a little cold weather?

Of course not, but twelve inches of snow is another story. Take another look at me, boss. How long do you think my legs are?

They look like about 12 inches, give or take an inch.

Exactly right, boss. Now your legs look like they're about 30 inches, so it's no problem for you to step through the snow, but for me it means making like a bunny rabbit and leaping over it. That can get pretty exhausting after a few hundred yards. Imagine my trying to do our usual three miles.

I guess your right, Vinnie. I never looked at it like that.

I can understand that, boss, it's been a long time since your legs were 12 inches long, and I'm sure you weren't walking in snow like this at that time. Heck, you probably weren't walking at all.

I don't know, Vinnie, that's been so long ago that my memory doesn't go that far. But you're right, even if I had wanted to walk in the snow then, I'm sure my mother would have had a different idea.

There's another problem with this snow which I'm sure you have never experienced.

Really? What's that?

Well, you see my tummy is built close to my legs, so walking in this stuff can really give the old tummy a shock. It gives a new meaning to the term "frozen food."

You're right again Vinnie. I never look at it that way.

So thanks for the invitation to go with you, boss, but I think I'm going to decline this time.

Perfectly understandable, Vinnie, and I'm glad we had this conversation.

You are?

Yes, it's like our Native Americans would say: "You never understand a person unless you walk two miles on their legs."

I like the Native American version better, but what do you say we go over to the gym and shoot some hoops?

REFLECTION:

Am I sensitive to the needs of those who may suffer from problems I have not experienced?
Am I helpful in assisting such people?
Is there some way I can call attention to these needs
    in places they are not met?

GRADUATION DAY

The children in our country are blessed to have the opportunity of receiving a good education. Teaching children is one of the best ways to share what we have received with others, and the rewards of a good education are a blessing to our families and our country. We all need to look back in thanksgiving for what we have learned and look for ways to use that learning for making our world better. We also need to continue learning, no matter how old we may be.

Why do all the children seem so happy, boss? I think it's because the end of the school year is coming and summer vacation is about to begin.

I guess that means we won't be seeing some of the children around so much anymore. They'll be graduating.

That's right, Vinnie. It's time to wish them well and send them on their way.

If I had a chance, there are some things I would like to say to them as they are graduating.

This is your chance, Vinnie, what words of wisdom do you have for them?

First of all, boss, I want to tell them how much they should appreciate the education they have received. They are very fortunate to have had an opportunity to get such a good education.

That's very true, Vinnie. I didn't know you appreciated the importance of a good education.

Oh, but I do, boss. If I had had an opportunity to go to school, I might have learned some things that would have helped me, like listening when I'm told not to chase things bigger and faster than me. Why, it's even conceivable that I could have learned to be a guide dog and helped someone who couldn't see. I know how important education is and I envy those young people who have learned so much. They have a great future.

What else would you tell them, Vinnie?

Secondly, I would tell them to be grateful to the people who made it possible for them to go to school. They should thank their parents and their teachers for doing such a good job and making the necessary sacrifices for them.

I agree with you a hundred percent, Vinnie. How would you suggest they thank them?

Just like I do, boss, by making good use of what they have learned.

You do that, Vinnie?

Sure. Haven't you noticed how I sit when told and shake hands when asked? Someone taught me those things and I try to put them to good use in getting extra treats.

Anything else you want to say to them?

Finally, I want to tell them to never stop learning. It's never too late to learn new things. That's something they try to pin on us dogs, saying that you can't teach us old dogs new tricks. That's poppycock!

I agree there, Vinnie. You never cease to amaze me with your unending creativity in learning new tricks.

Thanks, boss, I learned that from you.

You did?

Sure, look how much you're learning in your old age.

REFLECTION:

Take time to recall the happy memories of your own school days and give thanks to God for them.

List the ways you have been able to use the education you received.

What are you doing to continue your learning?

REST INSURED

Anxiety is a source of unrest and insecurity in our lives. We all search for ways to relieve this worry, sometimes in inappropriate ways. Many try to buffer themselves from worrying about their future by buying insurance to cover whatever crisis may come, but there is no insurance to protect us from life's setbacks and sorrows. We will find the only relief for problems that have no solutions is to place our trust in the One who will always provide for us. To paraphrase the Gospel, we pray: "I do trust in you, Lord, help my lack of trust."

What's that you're reading, boss?

It's a brochure explaining how I can get health insurance for you, Vinnie.

Why would you want health insurance for me, boss, I'm a perfectly healthy pooch?

Yes, but what if something were to happen to you? What would we do then?

You mean, if I should be hit by a car or truck?

Exactly, it has been known to happen, you know.

Yes, I think I remember, but it's still a little fuzzy. I think I got knocked on the noggin.

You sure did, and I had to take you to the hospital each time. That costs a little money, you know.

But I'm worth it, don't you think?

Sure you are, but if I had insurance, then the insurance would pay for your hospital costs.

It doesn't sound like a very good deal to me, boss. After all, I'm not planning to be hit by any cars again. Twice is enough.

Once is enough, Vinnie, but the way you chase after trucks and busses, I wouldn't be surprised if you were hit again.

I'll try to be more careful, boss.

That's good to know, but this insurance is good for more than just accidents.

Really? What else does it do?

Well, for example, if you got fleas, it would pay for the treatment to get rid of them.

I wonder what that would consist of, boss.

I don't know. Fortunately you've never had fleas, at least not to my knowledge.

You know what I say about fleas, boss.

What?

Easy come, easy flea.

Ohhhh! That's really bad Vinnie.

How much would this insurance cost you, boss?

It would be only $54.10 a month.

That seems like a lot of money just to cover getting hit in the head and taking care of the fleas I don't have.

It does more than that. It will also cover your vaccinations, illnesses, and annual check-ups.

Oh no, boss, let's just forget the whole thing. You buy that and you'll have me up at the doctor's office every time my nose gets warm. Besides, I don't need any more insurance.

What do you mean "any more?" You've never had any insurance.

Oh yes, I have. I've had you. What more do I need?

REFLECTION:

What problems have I encountered that have no human solutions?

Do I turn to prayer in the midst of my day to help me through the day?

Is my faith in God strong enough to let me believe that God will make a way?

Spend some time relaxing in the arms of your Father, feeling his abiding strength.

I'm a perfectly healthy pooch

INVISIBLE BUT REAL

We live in an age of science and technology. In such a time there is a tendency to question the very existence of those things which cannot be verified by measurements and experiment. It is a time in which the existence of God is questioned, along with other spiritual realities, which can be known only by faith. By faith, we accept and believe in those things which cannot be seen, and yet are real.

That's a strange sign in that yard, boss.

What's so strange about it, Vinnie?

It says there is a dog in training, but I don't see any dog.

If you look a little harder, Vinnie, you will notice that it also says invisible fence.

What does that mean?

It means that there is an invisible fence in that yard and the dog that lives there is learning how to use it.

I don't see any fence there.

That's why it's called an invisible fence.

Yes, but what good is an invisible fence? If I lived there I would just walk right through this so-called fence. After all, calling it a fence doesn't make it a fence.

Well, I have no doubt you would do exactly that, but you would soon learn that it wouldn't be a very good idea.

Why is that, boss?

Let's just say you would find it to be a very shocking experience and something you may not want to repeat.

What's so shocking about walking through a fence that doesn't exist? Are you feeling all right, boss? You're beginning to talk nonsense.

But the fence does exist, Vinnie. You just can't see it.

Well, if I can't see it then it isn't going to keep me from going through it, is it?

It may not keep you from going through it, but it would most dogs, and you're not like most dogs. You've been knocked silly chasing after cars, but you still chase after them, so this invisible fence may not do much good for you.

Very funny, boss, but why would a dog let a phony fence keep him from chasing cars, squirrels or anything else that caught his fancy?

Because, when he tries to cross this unseen fence, he is going to receive a little electric shock, just enough to make him not want to do it again.

Why didn't you say that in the first place, boss. Now I get it. So this invisible fence really exists; you just can't see it.

That's what I've been trying to tell you, Vinnie. Things you can't see do exist, even if you can't see them.

I knew that, boss. You don't have to get so huffy.

I'm not getting huffy, and why are you speeding up? What's the hurry?

I don't like that house. It's a dangerous place.

I don't see anything.

Well, boss, sometimes things exist even if you can't see them. Didn't you know that?

REFLECTION:

Do I find it hard to believe in what I have always been told is true?

How do I strengthen my faith in a time of faithlessness?

Have I felt any little "shocks" which help to reawaken my faith?

COUNT YOUR BLESSINGS

Irving Berlin had it right when he wrote: "If you're worried and you can't sleep, just count your blessings instead of sheep." We are blessed in so many ways, not only materially, but in our family, our faith, and the many conveniences of modern life. But these blessings are not universally shared, and there are many throughout the world and in our own country who need food, clothing and shelter, but more than anything—love. That is some we all can give, regardless of our station in life.

Is there anything wrong with you, Vinnie? You're awfully quiet.

I'm all right, boss, I'm just in a reflective mood. I was lying here looking out the window and counting sheep.

Counting sheep? What are you talking about? There aren't any sheep around here.

Hey, boss, where's your sense of humor? I'm not counting real sheep; I'm counting my blessings instead of sheep.

It's that time of year, isn't it Vinnie? A new year is just around the corner and now it's time to look back on the old year. It's been a good year, don't you think?

Boss, every year is a good year, if I can get up in the morning and take nourishment.

So what have you found as you look back over the year? Have you been able to put your paw on anything in particular for which you are grateful?

I sure have, boss, more things than I can count on my toes, and I have a lot of them—four feet, you know.

Would you mind sharing your thoughts with me?

Not at all, boss. First of all I am grateful for this warm house and a bowl of food and water each day. You know there are a lot of my relatives who never knew a house like this. They had to stay out of doors all the time and go looking for food. Some days they would go without eating. They would say I was living like a king, and come to think of it, I am.

It's interesting, isn't it Vinnie? We never stop to think of how well we live. There are so many in our world who would love to have just a roof over their heads and food to eat every day.

Yes, boss, and sometimes it bothers me that I, a dog, have more than some children. It just doesn't seem right.

Some things in our world aren't right, Vinnie.

That's the other thing, boss.

What's the other thing?

Like you say, some things in our world aren't right. But that doesn't mean they have to stay that way, does it?

No, I guess, not. So what are you suggesting?

Well, there's a new year just ahead of us. Why can't we use the new year to help make things righter?

You mean "more right?"

Right!

How are you going to do that?

I'm not sure, but if you and I put our heads together, I'll bet we come up with something.

Count me in, Vinnie, and Happy New Year!

REFLECTION:

Spend some time counting your blessings and give thanks to God.

Resolve to become more conscious of the spiritual and physical needs of others at home and abroad.

Seek out an agency whose work you would like to support.

LIVING BREAD

In the sixth chapter of St. John's gospel Jesus calls himself the bread of life and tells us that if we eat of this bread we will live forever. The bread Jesus speaks of is both the word he has spoken and the flesh and blood given in the Eucharist. We listen to God's word, spoken in Jesus, and we receive his body and blood in Holy Communion so that we can grow into the image and likeness of the God who created us. As humans we are tempted to live on bread alone, that is, the bread this world gives. The bread Jesus gives us draws us beyond what this world can give and fills us with the life which has no ending.

Ouch! You stepped on my foot, Vinnie.

Sorry, boss, I didn't mean to.

Anyway, what are you doing under the table?

I'm looking for anything you may have dropped. Sometimes I can find nice little treats under here.

Are you going to spend your whole life looking for treats, Vinnie? Haven't you anything better to do?

Not to my knowledge, boss. Do you have any ideas?

You know, Vinnie, there's more to life than eating. Some food nourishes our bodies, and some food nourishes our souls.

Is it important to nourish our souls, boss?

Nourishing our souls is just as important as nourishing our bodies, Vinnie. And sometimes spiritual nourishment, that's what we call food for our souls, is just as satisfying as food for our bodies.

Where do you find this spiritual nourishment, boss? I've never seen any under the table or in my food dish.

No you won't find it there, Vinnie. But that doesn't mean you haven't received any, because you have.

I have?

Yes, I've been giving you food for your soul by trying to share with you some of the lessons I've learned as a human. For example I've tried to teach you to be nice and gentle to everyone, even those you don't like.

How is that going to help, boss?

Well, actually, Vinnie, if you would listen to what I have to say to you when I share part of who I am with you, then you would become more and more like me. You would become almost like a human.

Gee, boss, that would be something. Imagine that: a dog acting like a human.

What about you, boss? You're already human. Where do you get this spiritual nourishment?

Just like you, Vinnie, I listen to the One who is more than human.

I know who that is, boss, that's Jesus.

Jesus said that if I eat the bread that he provides then I will have eternal life.

Is that better, boss?

That's the best, Vinnie. The more I listen to Jesus and learn from him, the more like Jesus I will be. That's eternal life.

You know what, boss? I'm glad I stepped on your foot. I learned a lot I might not have known.

REFLECTION:

Am I sufficiently attentive to the Word of God through my own reading or when in church?

Have I made any efforts to seek a better understanding of the Bible?

When I receive Holy Communion, am I attentive to what I am doing, or has it become too routine?

HEALTH CARE

Everybody is interested in maintaining their health and living well for as long as they can. People join health clubs, go on diets, take pills and submit to rigorous exercise programs, all in the hope of living longer and better. Maintaining our physical health is important, but maintaining our spiritual health is even more important. Just as a regular physical checkup is recommended, so too should a regular spiritual checkup be. Some have a spiritual director for that purpose and others make regular use of the sacrament of reconciliation.

See that house over there, Vinnie?
Uh-huh.

I think that's the one our former pastor and founder of our grade school, Fr. McGann, used to live in. He bought the house after he stopped being pastor at St. Vincent. I guess he didn't want to leave his parish.

That's nice, boss, but let's speed it up a little. That's not my favorite place.

Why not, Vinnie? It looks all right to me.

Yeah, well you know who has that house now, don't you?

You mean your doctor.

That's right, boss. She's very nice and I like her a lot, but I don't care for all those needles, and I really don't like getting weighed in.

But you need all those things, Vinnie. It's all part of maintaining your health and being able to live a good life. You have to admit, you've been very healthy all these years. No heartworms, no rabies, no parvo virus.

That's true, boss, but I still don't like getting stuck with all those needles and I don't understand why she has to know how much I weigh. That's very personal, you know.

Well, Vinnie, that's all part of staying healthy. I know it may not always be pleasant, but in the long run it's good for you.

But don't feel bad, Vinnie, people are the same way.

They are?

Oh yes. Sometimes we humans aren't very good about taking care of ourselves, Like you, we find it uncomfortable or inconvenient. And it's even harder for us, Vinnie, because we also have to take care of our souls.

You mean you have to do that too, boss?

Absolutely, Vinnie. We don't always behave the way we should and we get into bad habits. When that happens, we need to go and talk to the priest and tell him what's wrong with us. We call that confession.

So that's what you mean on Saturday morning when you tell me you're going to hear confessions.

Right, Vinnie.

Do people enjoy going to confession, boss?

I don't think so, Vinnie. Like your getting weighed, it's rather personal and hard to admit.

I can understand that, boss.

Yes, Vinnie, but going to confession is very important for maintaining our spiritual health. We don't like to do it, but when we have done so, we feel a whole lot better.

Can I tell you a little secret, boss?

Sure, what is it?

Well, the real reason I don't like getting weighed is that I know I'm going to have to go on a diet.

I know, Vinnie, and we don't like being told we have to stop sinning.

REFLECTION:

What am I doing to ensure my spiritual well being?

Do I get to confession or spiritual direction on a regular basis?

Do I make it a habit to daily examine my conscience?

I know I'm going to have to go on a diet

HELP WHERE HELP IS NEEDED

There are so many people in the world who have so little to live on. We are blessed to have not only food, but the benefits of care for our elderly and health care in our times of illness. The Church, with its worldwide outreach, is in an excellent position to remind us of those less fortunate than ourselves. And the Church, not burdened with a heavy overlay of bureaucracy, can channel our donations more directly to those in need.

Whoa, boss! What's that new piece of furniture in the sanctuary? I almost ran into it.

So I noticed. Maybe you ought to slow down a bit. Anyway, it's not a piece of furniture.

What is it, then?

It's a collection bin for donations to help the poor. We're collecting rice bowls.

Rice bowls? Why do you need rice bowls? I don't even like rice.

That's good, because they're not for you, and besides, we're not collecting rice.

What are you collecting then?

We're collecting rice bowls.

C'mon boss. Quit fooling around. Why do you want rice bowls, if you're not planning to put rice in them?

Let's back up here a bit, Vinnie. The rice bowls we are collecting are not really rice bowls.

Then what are they?

They're little cardboard banks people put money in to help poor people in other parts of the world.

I get it. You call them rice bowls because they help buy rice and food for hungry people.

You're amazing, Vinnie. But there's more to it than that.

There is?

Yes, you see, some people use rice bowl recipes to eat one meal a week similar to a meal a poor person in Africa or India might eat.

How does that do any good, boss?

The idea is that the poor person's meal is less expensive, so a family can take the money they save and put it in their rice bowl.

What a great idea, boss! A family offers up their fasting to help another. It kills two birds with one stone.

Right, Vinnie, but wait, there's more.

Tell me, boss, I'm all ears.

You see, it's not just rice that people need. For example, there's little Jenita in Angola. Because people were fighting there, health care workers could not visit her village with the necessary polio immunizations. Jenita contracted polio and lost the use of her legs. She could only crawl.

How did the rice bowls help her?

With Rice Bowl money health workers can immunize people like Jenita, and now Jenita has a wheelchair to move around the village.

What a neat idea this rice bowl thing is, I hope it works.

Me too. Hey, wait a minute, Vinnie, you left one of your biscuits lying next to the rice bowl basket.

Let's go, boss.

REFLECTION:

How generous have I been in helping the poor?

What would be a reasonable amount for me to consider on a regular basis?

What resources are available to help me become aware of the needs of third world nations?

EVERYBODY COUNTS

There are few pleasures comparable to knowing that you have been a positive force in the life of another. Welcoming the stranger has been an important part of the Judaeo-Christian tradition. We read of Abraham's welcoming the strangers, who as it turned out, were angels from heaven bringing him the good news that he, at last, was going to be a father. St. Benedict continued that tradition among his monks, insisting that hospitality be offered to all visitors. There are many strangers at the doors of our homes and cities, awaiting an invitation to be part of our lives.

Look over there , boss. It's a little kitten.

It sure is, Vinnie. I wonder what it's doing down here on the towpath.

It looks lost to me. Do you want me to go after it?

No, Vinnie, that won't be necessary.

I feel sorry for that little fella, boss. I don't think it has a home, and anything could happen to it down here. What if that fox gets it?

I agree, Vinnie. Maybe somebody will take it home with them.

What about us, boss? Why don't we take it home?

We'll have to think about that, Vinnie. Do you think you could share your house with a cat?

What do they eat, boss?

Cat food.

No problem then.

Did you ever have a cat, boss?

Oh yes, over a period of time I had three of them.

How did you get them?

Well, the first one, Juno, just showed up at the door and we began to feed it and before we knew it, we had a cat.

You called your cat Juno? That's a funny name for a cat.

Well, Juno was the queen of the gods, and that's the way that cat acted, like she was the queen of the house.

What happened to Juno?

She was chasing after a squirrel one day and was hit by a car and killed.

That's sad, boss, but I know what it's like to be hit by a car, and I can tell you, it's no fun.

Yes, but before that happened she had kittens. Cats have a way of doing that. We kept one of the kittens, whom we mistakenly named Apollo, another Greek god.

Why was that a mistake?

Because Apollo turned out to be a girl.

You said you had three cats.

Yes, the third one was Jupiter, the king of the gods. He was black like you and very beautiful. He was also very friendly like you. He would jump on my lap and watch television with me.

Golly, boss, you sure had a lot of cats. What ever possessed you to have so many?

Well, they just kind of crept up on me, and I took them in, and I'm glad I did. I enjoyed them and they were fun to have around. Cats can be very comical at times.

I'll say this for you, boss. You seem to collect a lot of strays. I guess I was one of them.

Yes, you were, Vinnie, and now we're all glad we have you. We've never been sorry we welcomed you little guys. You've been a blessing to us.

Ditto, boss, ditto!

REFLECTION:

What do I know about the homeless and what makes them homeless?

What services are available in my city or town to help the homeless?

How do I respond to those who come asking me for help?

HOME SWEET HOME

We live in a world and at a time when there are so many things we can buy to increase our comfort and our pleasure. Such a world tempts us to look in the wrong place for the things that are really important. All the money in the world cannot buy us peace and happiness. As the saying goes: "The best things in life are free." Friends and the wonderful world of nature are ours for the asking, and they cost us nothing but our attention and devotion.

Isn't this a great day for a ride, Vinnie?
It sure is, boss. Thanks for bringing me with you. Where are we going?

I thought we would go to the park for a hike. It will be a pleasant change from our walks through the city.

I'm all for that, boss. There are always some wonderful new sounds, sights and smells in the park.

You look so pensive, Vinnie. What are you thinking of?

Oh, nothing, boss. I was just taking in the scenery.

Do you see anything interesting out there?

As a matter of fact, I was looking at that building over there. It has an interesting name—The Dog Palace.

Oh that. Yes, it is interesting, isn't it? Do you know what it is?

I can't say that I do. What do they do there?

It's a dog hotel.

That's a pretty pretentious name for a dog hotel. Back in my day, we just called such a place a kennel.

And that's basically what the Dog Palace is. But it's a very different kind of kennel.

What's so different about it?

For one thing, you get your own room.

You mean, crate.

Oh no. It's more that just a crate. You get your own bed.

Big deal. What else?

How about a plasma TV?

You're joking, what in the world would I do with a plasma TV?

I don't know. I guess you could watch the animal channel.

No thanks. What else is there?

A swimming pool.

A swimming pool? Now you're getting down-right ridiculous. I don't even like to swim.

In that case, I guess you lie around the pool and sunbathe.

Very funny, boss. Now let's get down to the nitty-gritty. How's the food in that place?

I heard they serve you filet mignon.

Now you've got my interest. Didn't you say you're going on retreat this week? Where am I going to stay while you're gone?

It's up to you, Vinnie. Do you want to stay at the Dog Palace or at home with your friends?

I must admit, the filet mignon sounds attractive, but I think I'll stay home with the people who love me.

How much farther to the park?

REFLECTION:

What are the things that bring the most happiness into my life?

Have I ever purchased anything I would sacrifice one of those things for?

Just say a prayer of thanksgiving for the best gifts in your life.

WITH YOU ALWAYS

John Donne said: "Ask not for whom the bell tolls, it tolls for thee." We all know that we will face that diffi- cult hour of farewell at the end of our earthly life. We hope that there will be someone there with us to hold our hand and offer prayers. No one wants to expe- rience the death of a loved one, but when the time comes, it is so important that we walk those last few steps in the company of those we love. We should also let it be known that we want the presence of our spiri- tual guide, who can offer prayers together with us, at a time it may not possible for us to pray alone.

Time to go to bed, Vinnie. I'll see you in the morning.

OK, boss.

…..Is that you, boss? I thought you said you were going to bed.

I did go to bed, Vinnie.

So what are you doing up in the middle of the night?

I had a call from the hospital. Someone is dying and they need a priest.

I understand. If you don't mind, I'll wait for you here.

That'll be fine, Vinnie. I don't think they would let you in the hospital anyway.

Probably not. And boss, if you don't mind, there is no need for you to wake me when you get home. You can tell me about it in the morning.

Yeah, right.

.....Good morning, boss, how are you this morning?

A little sleepy, but I'll make it.

How did it go at the hospital last night?

It was a good thing I went, Vinnie. When I arrived at the patient's room, I found her all alone and very near death.

That's kind of sad, isn't it, boss? I don't think I would want to be all alone when I'm dying. I would want someone there to comfort me.

I agree, Vinnie. Nobody wants to die alone.

So why did they call you, boss? You didn't know that woman did you?

No, I didn't, but they wanted a priest to visit her before she died.

Why is that so important? I would want someone I know, not some stranger, if you don't mind my saying so.

No, not at all, Vinnie. You're absolutely right, but actually it's not me the person wants to see, it's the person I represent. They really want the presence of Jesus at a time as important as that.

That makes sense boss. I guess when people see a priest, they just think that Jesus is with them.

Yes, Vinnie. No matter how much a person prayed or didn't pray when they were well, they always want to know that God is with them at the time of their death.

It's like the saying: "There are no atheists in the foxhole."

That's right, Vinnie.

What do you say to a person at a time like that, boss? I don't think I would know what to do.

Sometimes there is nothing a person can say. Sometimes it's just important that you should be there, holding their hand and letting them know they're not alone.

Is that all you do, boss?

No, I also pray with them, and I know that they are praying with me. That's the most important part of all.

It sure is, boss. I'm glad you went last night. I wish I could go with you, but the next time I'll be sure to pray for them while you're gone.

REFLECTION:

Have I given any thought to what my desires are at the end of my life?

Have I asked my family to call the church at that time?

How can I best prepare for that moment even now?

ST. VINCENT PARISH

St. Vincent Parish is located on the crest of Akron's West Hill, rising from the valley which once formed the basin for the Ohio canal. The history of St. Vincent is intimately connected to the history of the Ohio canal, which linked Lake Erie and the Ohio River.

In the early part of the nineteenth century, Irish immigrants began to arrive in America in great numbers. Their flight was precipitated by the Potato Famine, which claimed the lives of many in their native land. Willing to work wherever work was to be found, many of the Irish helped build the canal which brought industry and trade to Akron, Ohio.

In 1837, the pastor of St. Francis Xavier Church in nearby Doylestown began to visit these Irish Catholics, celebrating Mass in their homes, until a frame church was built in 1844. Construction on the present church began in 1864, and after a suspension of efforts during the Civil War, was completed in 1867.

Akron's first Catholic school began here in 1853. The parish still has an elementary school, while the high school has now merged and is known as St. Vincent-St. Mary High School.

St. Vincent continues to be an active parish serving the spiritual needs of its parishioners and providing education for its youth. The hard work and sacrifices of its first members continue to the present time, and St. Vincent is proud to be the first Catholic Church in Akron, Ohio.

How did I do, boss?

Printed in the United States
203422BV00001B/142-1176/P